HOW TO SELL YOUR HOME IN TODAY'S MARKET

HOW TO SELL YOUR HOME IN TODAY'S MARKET

Sell Faster in the 21ST CENTURY

David and Victoria Ranck

Victoria and David Ranck
Visit our website at www.VictoriaRanck.com

Printed in the United States of America

First Printing: Dec 2018
David Ranck LLC

ISBN- 9781791731298

"Make sure every day you do what matters most. When you know what matters most, everything makes sense. When you don't know what matters most, anything makes sense."

— Gary Keller in "The ONE Thing: The Surprisingly Simple Truth Behind Extraordinary Results" (Keller, 2013)

This book is dedicated to

Frederick "Fred" Paul
And
Herbert "Bud" Ranck

Your journeys carried you away many years ago, but you
remain in our hearts and thoughts each and every day
The world was a better place while you were in it

Thank you for the love you gave
And the sacrifices you made
For your families

TABLE OF CONTENTS

PART ONE: WHERE ARE THE BUYERS?

The More Things Change, the More They Change.

"People make a lot of inferences, correct and incorrect, about houses that have been on the market for a long time" - Stan Humphries

It's true. Great homes don't always sell right away. When a home doesn't sell within a reasonable amount of time, a typical reaction is to determine that the price was too high or perhaps to blame it on "the Market". Setting the correct price is an especially important factor in making sure your home sells as quickly as you want but it is far from the only factor to consider.

Today's Real Estate market is unlike the market of only a few years ago. It is no longer enough to list a home in the MLS and on the big syndicated websites. Every home for sale is listed on these sites. You must make your home stand out in the crowd and put your listing in front of prospective buyers *where they are.* That means digital and social marketing combined with more traditional methods of getting the word out.

In this book, we provide up-to-date techniques designed to make sure your home sells at the right price and in the right amount of time. We also show you how to combine social media and Internet marketing with tried-and-true techniques that complement each other.

◆ ◆ ◆

THE GREAT EQUALIZER

Why We Wrote this Book

Knowledge is Power
– Francis Bacon

Tim Berners-Lee, a British scientist, invented the World Wide Web (WWW) in 1989, while working at CERN. Some years later while at a technical conference in Orlando, I attended a seminar on The Future of the Internet. The speaker spoke passionately about how the Internet could bring the power of information to everyone on the planet. The Internet would become the great equalizer.

Today we live in the world he described. The Internet has become ubiquitous in western civilization. The World Wide Web has brought a previously unimagined quantity of information to our computer screens, tablets and smartphones. We shop online, get medical advice online and yes, we find our next home online.

The purpose of this book is to teach you how to leverage the power of the Internet to reach potential buyers for your home. But placing a home for sale on the Internet is not enough. To find buyers where they are, you need to know how to reach them using Social Media combined with traditional advertising.

WHO IS THIS BOOK FOR?

We wrote this book for homeowners, both those who have decided to sell their homes and those that have already tried to sell their home without success. You will find essential information that will guide you through the process of selling your home: from the first steps of preparing your home for sale, all the way through to when your home under is contract. You'll have the tools and techniques to sell your home in today's technology-driven world, so your home doesn't sit on the market month after month after month, losing money.

If you have been trying to sell your home, either on your own or with the assistance of a Realtor and it hasn't sold in a reasonable amount of time, you will find ideas in this book you and your Realtor can use right now to get your home sold. If other homes are selling and your home hasn't sold, you probably wonder why your home has been sitting on the market. We'll help you find the reason (or reasons) that your home is not winning the competition. Once you have a good idea what is preventing your home from selling, you'll be able to make the changes that will bring qualified buyers who want to buy your home.

If you aren't sure that you want to sell your home, understanding the principles we outline here will help you decide if now is the right time for you to sell. Will the market support the price you need or want to get? What can you do to maximize the selling price of your home? Would it be advisable to wait "for the market to get better"?

HOW TO USE THIS BOOK

We have divided this book into three sections:
- PART ONE: Where Are the Buyers?
- PART TWO: Winning the Competition
- PART THREE: New Tools for a New Market

My best suggestion is that you fight the temptation to skip ahead and read the book through from start to finish. If you skip to the "fun" part -using technology – you will miss ingredients vital to your success.

The first section describes why new techniques are required to effectively reach buyers in today's market. The second section lays out the essential steps you must take before you put your home on the market. Buyers today shop at the speed of light and if your home does not present well on the Internet, Mobile Devices and Social Media, they will blow right past it without giving it so much as a glance.

The third section lays out a plan for leveraging technology and traditional marketing synergistically to get your home sold. We describe the marketing plan we follow with our own clients. You and your Realtor can review these ideas together and implement the ones that will be most effective for you.

Let's get started!

WHAT YOU WILL LEARN

In this book, we begin with the fundamental steps that must be taken for a home to sell in today's digital world. Most of these principles aren't new at all, but they have assumed an even greater measure of importance because of the way buyers find homes today. In the section on the use of technology to get in front of the right buyers, we explain some of the up-to-date marketing techniques we employ for our own clients.

Here's a sample of what you will learn in the following pages:

- How the Real Estate Market Has Changed
- How Buyers Look for Homes Today
- Finding Buyers Where They Are
- How to Decide on the Right List Price
- What Makes Buyers Choose One Home Over Another
- Simple Things You Can Do to Prepare Your Home for Sale
- The Importance of Using Up-to-Date Marketing Techniques
- How to leverage Social Media to Help Sell Your Home

This isn't a book based on theory – it is grounded in real-world results and industry statistics. You'll be armed with information on how to leverage technology to get a leg up on the competition. We've included Case Studies that showcase examples of homes that didn't sell at first and how they were eventually sold using the techniques in this book. We'll also discuss how to go about finding the right Realtor to partner with to sell your home. We have included questions for you to ask Realtors during the interview process, so you have the knowledge to select a top-notch Realtor who can leverage modern techniques to sell your home for the best price in the right amount of time.

David and Victoria Ranck

A CHANGING MARKET

*How the Real Estate Market Has
Changed and Why*

*Change is inevitable. Change is constant. –
Benjamin Disraeli*

Change is inevitable. Not that long ago if you wanted to look for a home you drove to the local Realtor's office and told the person at the front desk you were looking to buy a new home. She/he would take you to a Realtor who would bring out "The Huge Book" which held all the active listings in the area. You would then spend hours poring over pages and pages of listings to hopefully find a few that you might like. Not all the homes for sale were listed in the book but it was a way to start looking. If you wanted to look for a home on your own, you went to the newspaper before you went to the Realtor.

When you put your home up for sale, it was added to the same massive book which was distributed to all the Real Estate offices in the area. Your Realtor may or may not advertise your home in the Realty section of the local newspaper. Newspaper advertising was expensive, even in those days. Of course, if your home had a higher price point it may have been featured in a larger newspaper ad or even in a full-page advertisement. But a Realtor could only advertise a relatively few number of homes each week because of the cost. Buyers didn't have a reliable way to find your home and they really needed to come into a Realtor's office if they wanted to see all the available listings.

ENTER THE INTERNET

Then along came this new-fangled idea called the "Internet" that changed everything. Those incredibly large listing books were replaced by what we call the Multiple Listing Service or MLS. There are many Multiple Listing Services throughout the country, but they all post their *member's* listings on the Internet.

I (David) had the privilege of helping to design and implement a prototype of one of the very first Internet-based MLS systems. At the time I was a software engineer in Baltimore Maryland. We built in features that we take for granted today – things like automated feeds of homes for sale based on a buyer's needs and sophisticated parameterized search to help Realtors find the right home for their buyers. We even pioneered what we called "email push" which sent buyers an email containing a list of homes matching their criteria as soon as the homes hit the market. We thought we were really cool – and we were, for that time period!

Piggy-backing on the web-based MLS, big syndicated sites like Zillow and Realtor.com began to arise. These sites made it much easier for potential buyers to search for homes from the comfort of their home and when they found a home they wanted to see, they could contact a Realtor to set up a personal showing.

Today virtually every home that is available for sale (unless the owners are selling it themselves) is on the MLS and on the big syndicated sites. Almost all Realtors list their homes for sale on the MLS and of course they put a sign in the yard, but many times that's where the "marketing" ends. In today's world that just isn't enough.

MOBILE DEVICES

The next revolution in the Real Estate market came with the widespread adoption of mobile devices such as smart phones and tablets. Many people today don't own a traditional computer or laptop. All their web browsing and online commerce is accomplished on their phone or tablet. An older couple recently evidenced this when we listed their home. You might not think that they would be technically savvy, and they really weren't very sophisticated in their use of technology in general. And yet they made heavy use of their smart phones for web browsing, email and more. They had no problem e-Signing contract documents with their smartphone when a buyer purchased their home.

Age alone is not a good indicator of how adept someone is at leveraging mobile devices for everyday tasks. As you might expect the millennial generation is practically physically attached to their phones. According to a recent Pew Research Center Report, 20% of adults in the U.S. use smartphones instead of Broadband Internet. The percentage is higher with young adults 18-29 (28%) but 10% of adults over 65 use a smartphone for online access exclusively (Mobile Fact Sheet, 2016). This trend is likely to continue to rise.

SOCIAL MEDIA

The rise of Social Media such as Facebook, Instagram and YouTube is another important factor in the change of the Real Estate market. Home buyers don't generally search for homes on social media, with the notable exception of sites like Nextdoor.com. The majority of Americans use social media sites today. 68% of Americans are on Facebook and 73% of us use YouTube (Social Media Use in 2018, 2018). Facebook remains the primary platform for interactive connections, but younger users are also leveraging networks such as Instagram, Snapchat, and Twitter in larger numbers.

Of the over two-thirds of the U.S. that are Facebook users, roughly three-quarters visit Facebook at least once a day. About one half of Facebook users say they visit the site several times each day. We aren't just talking about young kids, either. 66% of adults between 50 and 64 are on Facebook. While the video-sharing site YouTube is not a "traditional" Social Media site, it has many social elements. Over three-quarters of Americans use YouTube today and they watch over 5 billion videos EACH DAY! (YouTube by the Numbers, 2018)

If home buyers aren't searching for homes on Social Media sites, why is this important? Because most Americans spend a significant amount of time on sites like Facebook every day! If you want to sell your home, it stands to reason that finding a way for Facebook users to see it is an incredibly good idea.

SUMMARY

Gone are the days when a Realtor can list a home on MLS, put a sign in the yard and expect the home to sell quickly and at the right price. Unfortunately, in many cases that is exactly what is done. If your home is going to rise to the top of the many choices buyers have on the Internet, you need to do something different. How can your home stand out among the competition? Your home needs to go where buyers are. Yes, buyers are searching on the Internet using their laptops and phones, but how can your home cut through all the noise and reach *interested* buyers? Before we answer those questions, we need to know how buyers find homes in today's market.

KEY TAKE-AWAYS

- Technology has forever changed the Real Estate market

- Simply putting a home for sale on the MLS is not be enough

- Your home needs to stand out among the online noise

- Social Media is a ready-made audience when you want to sell your home

HOW BUYERS FIND HOMES TODAY

They Aren't Looking in the Newspaper

I don't think people understand the power of social media or our phones. – Zendaya

Last weekend I was holding an open house at one of our listings and had a good number of potential buyers turn out that Sunday afternoon. As part of my dialogue with visitors I ask them how they found the open house. Not one person said they came that day because of the many signs I had placed on nearby busy intersections and street corners. Every single person said they came because they saw the open house listed on the internet or they saw it on social media. We know that internet sites and social media are of primary importance when marketing homes today, but to my knowledge this was the first time that *every single visitor* at one of our open houses found the open house through these media outlets.

If you want to sell your home, you need to go where the buyers are. Years ago, a common mistake of new small business owners was to assume that placing a Yellow Pages ad was all that was needed to bring customers flocking into their shop. Victoria and I had a retail shop back then and thankfully we took the time to study marketing techniques for small businesses. The author of one book that we read talked about what he called "Shotgun Marketing". Essentially, he was saying that business owners needed to put their message in front of their potential customers where they were. At that time, it meant creating mailers, placing small signs along neighborhood roads, radio ads and so on. The key was to go to customers *where they spent their time* – in the car on the way to work, in their neighborhood as they came home from work or while they relaxed at home. Where do think today's home buyers spend much of their time when they are looking for a house?

THE HOME SEARCH PROCESS

How Buyers Searched For Homes 2018

Source	Percentage
Online Website	93%
Real Estate Agent	86%
Mobile or Tablet	73%
Open House	53%
Yard Sign	46%
Online Video	37%
Print	13%

(Profile of Home Buyers and Sellers 2018, 2018)

As we can see from the graph above, the vast majority of home buyers are leveraging the Internet, Mobile Devices and Realtors to look for their next home. This is true across all age groups. 82% of home buyers aged 65 and older used the Internet in their search for a home. Mobile devices have become an integral part of the home search process for most buyers. Print media usage continues to fall while other traditional search methods such as open houses and yard signs continue to be important sources used in the search process.

According the National Association of Realtors (NAR):

"The typical buyer used a mobile device to search for properties online. S/he looked at websites with photos, home listings and information about the home buying process. S/he then contacted an agent and visited a median of 10 homes over 10 weeks before purchasing a home." (Real Estate in a Digital Age 2017, 2017)

These statistics indicate that it is wise to make your home as available as possible, in as many ways as possible to buyers searching online. The sheer number of listings online also makes it important to find a way to make your home stand out among the online crowd, so it gets noticed. According to Tribute Media, a website has 7 seconds to grab a visitor's attention (7 Seconds, 2017). Mobile users may have an even shorter attention span since they can flip between online listings with a mere flick of their finger. Once they skip a home because it didn't grab their attention quickly enough, they will probably never see it again.

After they used the Internet to search for their home, 89% of the time buyers purchased the home they found through a Realtor. 5% purchased directly from a builder, 3% bought a home directly from someone they knew and 2% purchased a home for sale by owner from someone they did not know (Profile of Home Buyers and Sellers 2018, 2018).

HOW BUYERS SCORE YOUR HOME

Today's buyers don't have to visit a home to learn what it's like to live in the neighborhood. They don't have to visit the schools, drive through the area to find the closest shopping or walk around the property to judge how noisy or quiet it is. These values are now qualitatively rated online. Buyers can simply look at the numbers.

Walk Score
https://www.walkscore.com/

Walk Score uses your address to generate a score from 1 to 100, higher scores indicate that it is easier to get around your neighborhood without a vehicle. How easy can someone walk to dining, grocery shopping, parks, schools or entertainment?

More important than the technology, though, is the idea that Walk Score has quantified walkability, taken an abstract quality—you know it when you see it, sort of—and turned it into something that can be measured against other addresses, other neighborhoods, even other cities .... Walk Score gets people thinking concretely about walking – Slate (Vanderbilt, 2012)

What if your home doesn't have a great walk score? Not everyone is looking for a home that's tucked right in the middle of everything. Many buyers are looking for a home in a quieter area. A lower walk score isn't necessarily a bad thing. If your home is in an area with a high walk score, you'll want to talk it up in your Lifestyle Narrative.

Soundscore
http://howloud.com/soundscore/

Soundscore rates an address with a score of from 50 (very loud) to 100 (very quiet). It displays the scores on a heat map. Low noise levels attract buyers that are looking for peace and quiet while those that want to be in the middle of the action might not care about the sound score. If your home has a good sound score (above 70), consider putting that in your listing description and Lifestyle Narrative. You could say something like "A Sound Score of 77 means you can sip a glass of wine on the lanai and enjoy the peaceful surroundings after a long day at work". If your home has a lower sound score, it may be that it is in an area where there is a lot of exciting nightlife or it has highway access nearby. Turn the lower score into a positive feature.

GreatSchools
https://www.greatschools.org/

Families seek the areas that have the best schools. GreatSchools rates an area's schools on a scale of 1 to 10 with 1 being below average, 5 being average and 10 above average. When a buyer enters an address into the site's search bar, they are shown the assigned schools for the address. They can even view all the homes for sale in the area. One caveat: you can't put this data in your listing.

KEY TAKE-AWAYS

- Almost all of today's buyers use the Internet in the search for a new home

- Most home buyers use mobile devices and/or phones

- Buyers still depend on Realtors to help them find the perfect home

- The attention span of a home buyer searching online or on their phone is *very* short

- Once they decide to purchase a home, the vast majority of buyers use a Realtor to complete the purchase

DON'T IGNORE THIS RULE

The Pareto Principle

Getting bigger results is all about focusing on that 20 percent – Gary Keller

Vilfredo Pareto was an Italian economist who lived in the late 1800s. He noticed that 80% of the land in Italy was owned by 20% of the people. He then carried out surveys in other countries and found that there was a similar distribution of land ownership. This ratio has been found to apply to a wide number of scenarios, from software development to sports. For example, in 2018 20% of the top earners in the U.S. will pay roughly 80% of the Federal taxes (Top 20% of Americans Will Pay 87% of Income Tax, 2018). Microsoft found that if they fixed 20% of the most-reported software bugs, they would eliminate 80% of the errors and system crashes (Microsoft's CEO: 80-20 Rule Applies To Bugs, Not Just Features, 2002).

What does this have to do with successfully selling a home? The 80/20 rule states that 80% of the results will come from just 20% of the action taken. A wise application of the 80/20 rule can save you time and effort in selling your home. We mentioned earlier that we need to find a way for your home to stand out among all the online noise and rise to the top of the pack. We recommend that you concentrate on highlighting the 20% of your home's features that make it special. The rest of the 80% are still important and shouldn't be ignored, but in photos, videos and listing descriptions we want to feature the elements that make your home special.

We sometimes call this your Unique Selling Proposition. These features aren't the common ones that your home shares with all the other homes with which you are in competition. Do you remember that online buyers have at most a 7 second attention span? The 20% are the features that will grab a buyer's attention and get them to sit up and take notice of your home over and above the others on the market.

THE 80/20 RULE IN ACTION

Buyers are looking for your home's unique features. When preparing your home for sale, concentrate on and improve if necessary, the unique features of your home. If your home has a beautiful view, find a way to accentuate it by artfully staging the lanai. If the wonderful view is hampered by dirty floor-to-ceiling windows, make sure they are spotlessly clean before photos are taken and the home is shown to buyers. If your home's landscaping is one of its best features, make sure you add new mulch, trim plants, keep the pathways clear of fallen leaves and so on.

Every home has its unique features. If you aren't sure of yours, here are a few suggestions to think about:

- A beachfront or waterfront location offering a spectacular view
- Open fields frequented by wildlife
- A pond that is home to egrets and herons
- Nearby walking or biking trails
- Sunset or sunrise views
- A fenced-in yard for your dogs (something that isn't always easy to find in Southwest Florida)
- A private, secluded location
- A custom, heated saltwater pool with a waterfall
- Mature trees and landscaping
- A "bonus room" not found in other homes in the area
- A truly gourmet kitchen

- A home that is FULLY renovated, and move-in ready
- Proximity to shopping, the arts or dining

What happens if you don't concentrate on the 20% that really matters? In that case you are showcasing the same things your home shares with every other similar home on the market. How well do you think your home will stand out against the competition if you don't concentrate on its uniqueness? Not showcasing the right things also means that effort is unnecessarily wasted. It usually means that the 80% gets done, which has minimal effect and the most effective 20% remains undone.

Sometimes homeowners are fixated on something about their home that means a lot to them but that may not mean that much to potential buyers. When they allow this to happen, they normally miss something important that could result in a quicker sale or a higher price. Don't bother paying an electrician lots of $$$$ to change out ceiling lights with new fixtures that are marginally "better" when the front door is badly in need of repainting.

Remember that buyers need to be motivated to buy. Most people are motivated by emotion not logic. Simple, easy things like changing paint colors or weeding the garden may have a greater effect than things that require much more effort. Try to remove your emotions from the picture and see things from the perspective of the potential buyer. We walk through a client's home and make a "punch list" of the 20% items that we know will make the home most saleable to buyers. We have an objective viewpoint because we aren't emotionally tied to the home and we also know from experience what things to concentrate on. If you have extra time and want to work on some of the 80%, go ahead – but only after the 20% is done.

MARKET THE 20%

Following the 80/20 rule helps you in two ways. First it can help to make sure that you grab the right buyer's attention when they first see your home online and again when they come in for a private showing or open house. It also helps to weed out buyers who wouldn't be interested in your home even if they saw it in person. Your home will be shown to the people that are most likely to be motivated to make an offer.

We'll discuss the details of marketing your home later, but for now it is important to understand that you'll want to focus in on the 20% of marketing that will have the most impact. Ensure that buyers will notice your home's most important and unique features. This starts with the photography. I can't emphasize enough how important it is that a Professional Real Estate Photographer be hired to shoot the photos of your home. We make sure that the photographer captures these unique features and then we prominently display those photos in the online listing and property web page.

While photos and videos are vital to grab buyer's attention quickly, once we have their attention, we want to draw them in by accentuating your home's features. We call this the Lifestyle Story. We craft a one-of-a-kind Lifestyle Story for every home that we list. It focuses on creating emotion in the buyer fueled by your home's unique features, its 20%. We'll talk more about the Lifestyle Story later.

CASE STUDY #1:
"I DON'T KNOW WHY THIS HOME WON'T SELL!"

Last year I was talking to a Realtor that had a home for sale in a sought-after neighborhood not far from where Victoria and I live. The home was offered at a price that was in line with other, similar homes. She couldn't understand why the home was getting almost no showings. She showcased the home at a meeting of the local Realtor Association and bemoaned her plight. When the pictures of the home were shown to us on the projection screen, I nearly fell out of my seat. The pictures weren't bad, they were *horrible*! The Realtor had taken the photos with her smartphone, had used inadequate lighting and had done no staging or decluttering of the home whatsoever. The home looked dark, dreary and uncared for. Had she taken the time to remove the clutter, do a little staging and to hire a Professional Photographer, it would have made all the difference in the world. The home would have had a MUCH higher chance of selling quickly and at a good price.

KEY TAKE-AWAYS

- Understand and apply the 80/20 rule to preparing your home for sale

- Focus on the 20% that will have the biggest impact on the sale of your home

- Find your home's unique features and showcase those features

- Market those features in all your collateral, online and off

PART TWO: WINNING THE COMPETITION

When You Sell Your Home You Are Entering a Competition

The healthiest competition occurs when average people win by putting above average effort
- Colin Powell

You've discovered your home's unique features, its 20%, its unique selling Proposition. Now that you know this, what are the most important things you can do to ensure your home sells at a good price in a reasonable amount of time? In this section we'll examine the vital components, the ingredients of a successful home sale. If you implement all the items we are about to lay out for you, your home will have the best chance of selling in relation to the competitors.

I chose the word "Competition" because it is important that you fully understand that you are entering a contest. Buyers have multiple choices besides your home. If your home doesn't beat the competition in some way, whether it's price, features, location, or something else, it won't sell quickly or won't sell for the best price possible.

There are many factors that affect the sale of a home, but these are the most important ones to concentrate on:

- Price and Features
- Condition
- Appearance
- Marketing

I've placed price and features together because we can't really talk about price without talking about the home's features. Usually we can't change the major features of a home to sell it. For example, your home is either located on a lake or it isn't. Condition and appearance also affect price and we'll discuss how much they affect price when we get there. Make sure your home wins the competition.

PRICING YOUR HOME TO SELL

The First Step to Winning the Competition

Price is what you pay. Value is what you get
- Warren Buffett

When a home doesn't sell, the knee-jerk reaction is often to assume it is priced too high. As we've already seen, that is not always the case. Even so, of all the ingredients we outlined above, price is absolutely the most important one. A price that is set too high will prevent buyers from even looking at the home online, much less in person. On the other hand, a price that is too low will leave money on the table. Proper pricing is the biggest tool you have to successfully market your home and beat the competition.

How do you arrive at the *best* price for your home? We've put together a short video that hits the highlights of this chapter. You can view it here:

MEET THE COMPETITION

Let's say you want to buy a new car. You go to the car dealer and you find the exact model you want. It is even the color you are hoping for. The dealer tells you that the price is $25,000. However, you are a good shopper, so you decide to go to another dealer in the next town. At the second dealer you find the same model car in the same color at the same price, $25,000. This car though has an upgrade package installed which includes a better sound system, leather seats and more. The upgrade package is worth $2,000.

Which car would you buy?

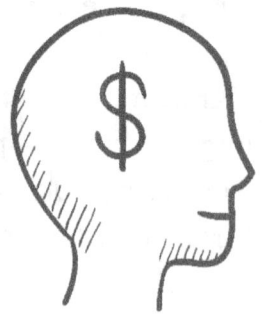

If you're like most people, you chose the second car. Why did you choose that one? Right. You chose it because you are getting more for your money. Everyone wants to feel they are getting the most for the money they are spending.

Now let's say you really didn't care about the upgraded sound system, the leather seats and the other upgrades. In fact, you don't want them at all. You decide to go back to the first dealer again.

What would you want the first dealer to do?

Right! You would want him to discount the car $2000! Home buyers are just like you. They look for the home with most features for the price, or they look for the home with the lowest price. Either way, it is ultimately all about price and features.

Ok. Now let's look at 3 different homes. Each of the following homes has similar features and location. They all have three bedrooms, two baths, a heated pool and an upgraded kitchen.

- Home #1 is listed at $349,000
- Home #2 is listed at $325,000
- Home #3 is listed at $299,000

Which home would you buy? Of course, you would choose home #3 which is priced at $299,000. And why did you choose that one? Because it has the same features as the other two homes for less money.

Now let's say that only home #2 had a pool and you really wanted a home with a pool. Now which home would you choose? You might still choose #3 because it is offered at a lower price, but you likely would choose #2. Why? Because the $26,000 difference in price is probably less than the cost of adding the pool that you really want.

One more scenario. This time let's say #1 is the only home with a pool. Would you buy this one because you really, really want that pool? Maybe, but if the cost of adding a pool is about $35,000 you might decide to buy the lowest price home. You could then add a pool and still come out ahead on price.

This is what we call *Value in the Eyes of the Buyer*. We also call it Perceived Value. What we mean by that is the buyer's perception determines the value of the home to them. You or I might look at things differently and for many good reasons. What matters in the end is not the value that you or I place on the home and features. The only value that matters is the buyer's Perceived Value. Which brings up an especially important point: You or your Realtor do not set the selling price of the home – the Market does.

MARKET ANALYSIS

How do you arrive at the right price then? If the buyer's perception of value ultimately determines the selling price of your home, how do you calculate what's in the mind of a buyer you haven't even met? You must understand the market and specifically you must know the local market. What types of homes having been selling best lately? What are the most active price points? To help arrive at the right list price for your home, you want to find homes like yours, in the same location that are currently for sale and that have recently sold. We call this a Comparative Market Analysis or CMA.

> *"The CMA is used to help evaluate how your home will fare against the competition. It takes a look at both homes that are currently listed and those recently sold. The purpose is to find the highest price that will still make the home competitive on the open market."* (Understanding The Comparative Market Analysis, 2013)

When a CMA is created, great care must be taken that ALL the features of a home, tangible and intangible, that matter to buyers in the current market are part of the comparison. It is not enough to look only at the number of rooms or the general condition of the home. Property location (e.g. a corner lot or a lake view), access to recreational areas, the quality of the schools, proximity to the beaches, even the facing of the home can be important inputs to the comparison. Is the landscape mature? What are the taxes? Is there a CDD fee? Is there an alarm system? How old is the AC and the roof? What appliances are included? Is natural gas available? What are the HOA regulations like? Can I park my motor home in the driveway? Can I prevent my neighbor from parking a motor home in his driveway? The list goes on and on.

When we create a CMA for a client, we take as many of the relevant factors into consideration as is practical. We start by looking for homes with similar features and then we use our local knowledge and experience to factor in more subtle things. It really is part art and part science.

One more point about creating a CMA. Sometimes you find a home that sold for an abnormally high or low price compared to most of the other homes that sold in the same time frame and in the same area. Or there may be a home currently on the market that is offered at a much lower price than other homes. When we see this, we ask ourselves what may have caused such a marked difference in price. Sometimes a home has been "stigmatized" because it's been on the market for so long and buyers think there must be something wrong with it. Or perhaps a home that sold far above the market value was sold to a family member and there are unknown factors that artificially pushed the price up. In that case the high sale price may be an anomaly and should be taken with a grain of salt.

A word of caution about online home evaluations. Many Realty websites and Realtors have a home evaluation page where you enter your address and the system generates a CMA automatically.

We have one of these online tools too. Just don't place the same value on a computer-generated CMA as you would on a CMA that was hand-crafted by a Realtor who knows what they are doing. We use the online CMA only as a fast, pre-evaluation tool. We never use it when listing a home. We always take the time and put in the work to create a custom CMA that takes the harder to qualify factors into account.

Since we mentioned online CMAs, what about the home value estimates on the big syndicated sites? I'll bet you can guess what I'm about to say. Yes, they are simply computer-generated CMAs that can't consider factors such as lot location, a view of a lake, or mature landscaping. Just like other online CMAs they are only useful for a quick estimate of your home's value. Just don't be surprised if a knowledgeable Realtor provides you with a custom CMA that is markedly different from the computerized CMA on the syndicated site.

MARKET VALUE

What role does fair market value play when setting the right price for your home? A common misconception is that if you want to sell your home for the most money you need to set the price extremely high because buyers are going to negotiate the price down. It may be hard to believe but setting a price that is too high can result in a LOWER selling price in the end.

The following diagram illustrates the effect of the price of a home on the number of buyers that will look for the property. As the price exceeds market value, the interest of potential buyers quickly wanes. Of course, the opposite is true as well. A price that is well below fair market value usually attracts many buyers. Unless you need to sell your home very quickly, this is probably not what you are looking for.

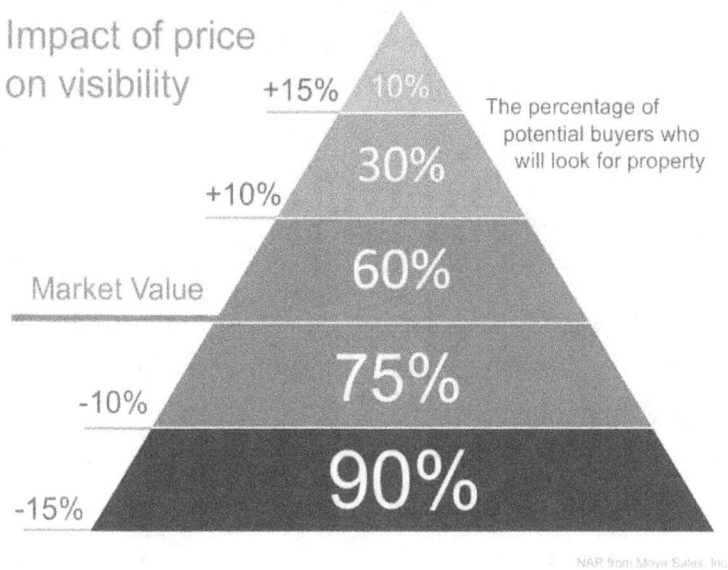

Impact of price on visibility

+15% | 10%
+10% | 30%
Market Value | 60%
-10% | 75%
-15% | 90%

The percentage of potential buyers who will look for property

NAR from Move Sales, Inc.

The place you want to be is near market value. In the Sarasota, Florida market most homes sell for about 95% of the asking price. Once you determine the market value of your home, you can use that ratio to help set the list price. If comparable homes are selling for $385,000 you might list your home at $399,000. All things being equal, your home may sell for about $385,000. This presumes that you know the market value of your home.

When you price your home properly you maximize the number of potential buyers that will view your home online and then request a showing or come to an open house. I can't stress this next point strongly enough. The single best opportunity you have to grab a buyer's interest is when your home first comes on the market. When the price is set too far above market value, many potential buyers won't give it a second look. And as we've previously discovered, the vast majority of buyers search for their next home online. With a swipe of their finger they'll instantly move on if your home is listed above their price range. Reducing the price later is certainly an option, but you will never have as broad an audience as when your home was first listed.

The activity around a listing is far greater when it first comes online. After the initial blur of activity, things level out. If a price reduction or other major change is made, we'll see another short blip of activity but nowhere near as much as in the first few days after going live.

The graph above shows the actual number of times a real-world listing was returned in search results on one of the syndication sites. When the listing first went active, it received over 13,000 views in the first week. By week 2 the number of times the listing was returned in search results dropped to about 4,000 and it dropped further in weeks 3 through 5.

What is the lesson here? If you want to reach the highest number of buyers that are interested in your home, you must price it right. If a home is priced too high, the best potential buyers may never see it online. Reducing the price can help to put it in front of the right buyers, but a price reduction is a suboptimal solution. For one thing, the initial flood of buyers that searched for a home will almost always be significantly larger than the smaller blip caused when the price is reduced. Price reductions need to be taken when required and should not be put off, but they are not a substitute for smart pricing in the first place.

In the next section we're going to look at the relationship between a home's condition and features and the price it can command.

CASE STUDY #2
MY HOME IS BETTER THAN ALL
OF THE OTHERS

This just happened this year. Victoria went on an appointment to list a home in a beautiful neighborhood in Sarasota. We've sold many homes in the area and know the market extremely well. She previewed the home and presented the owners with a hand-crafted CMA. The home had been partially updated but not all rooms had been remodeled. It had a great view of a golf course. There were a few minor things that Victoria felt held the home back from commanding top dollar. In addition, there were a few easy changes that could be made to enhance the home's value or at least help the home to sell more quickly.

Similar homes that had more complete upgrades and great views were selling in the $250,000 range. Victoria suggested that the home be listed for $269,000 and that the owner make the small changes she suggested. The owner was very adamant that her home was worth well over $300,000 and that she would not make any of the changes mentioned by Victoria. When asked why she thought her home was worth such a high price, she answered "Because my home is the best."

Not surprisingly she hired a different Realtor who listed her home at around $300,000. Predictably the home sat on the market and had few showings. The price was lowered a few times and the Realtor even offered a higher than usual commission to any agents that would bring a buyer. Eventually the price was lowered to $269,900, the same price suggested by Victoria. After 6 months with no offers, the listing agreement with the original agent expired and the owner hired a new agent.

The new agent also advised the owners to make a few small changes and now the owners were under a bit of time pressure to sell their home. They made some of the changes and listed the home at $250,000. The price was reduced to $240,000 after several weeks. The home finally sold almost one year after Victoria originally met with the owner for $227,000 - $33,000 less than it would have probably sold for with the list price Victoria suggested.

David and Victoria Ranck

THE 4 VALUES OF YOUR HOME

A buyer makes an offer on your home and you agree to sell it to her for $400,000. The bank's appraiser values the home at $380,000 and when you check the tax records, you find your home has been assessed at $320,000. But one of the big syndicated sites said your home was worth $420,000. What is going on here!

The differences in these home evaluations can be very confusing to buyers and sellers alike. Why is there such a disparity between these numbers? Does it matter that the assessed value is so much less than the selling price? The reason the numbers are so far apart is that they are calculated differently and serve different purposes.

Fair Market Value

This is the price that a willing and able buyer will pay for your home. It is a range, not a single number since the amount can vary from buyer to buyer.

Appraised Value

This is the value of your home as determined by an appraiser for the purposes of obtaining a mortgage. It could be more or less than the market value. If the appraised value is less than the selling price of the home, the buyer may have trouble obtaining financing. The bank needs to ensure that if the buyer defaults on the mortgage, they will be able to recoup their investment in the home.

Assessed Value

The assessed value is determined by the county tax assessor for the purpose of taxation. In many cases this value will be less, sometimes much less, than the market value. In our area the assessed value is usually about 80% of the fair market value. The difference between the assessed value and the market value is called the "Equalization Rate".

Automated Evaluation

We mentioned earlier that the value as determined by automated CMA tools is not always accurate. In fact, it can be incredibly inaccurate! Why is that? The online automated program cannot visit your home and see the wonderful view you have from your lanai. It also can't hear the overwhelming road noise in the other guy's home two neighborhoods away from yours.

What if the appraisal comes in lower than the selling price of my home? Can the buyer still get a mortgage? Maybe. If the selling price is $400,000, the buyer has a down payment of $40,000 and the appraisal comes in at $380,000 the buyer would need to come up with extra cash. The bank is agreeing to loan 90% of the value of the home. 90% of $380,000 is $342,000. The buyers would need to come up with an additional $18,000 over their original down payment amount of $40,000 ($400,000 - $342,000 = $58,000).

Appraisals can be challenged. A list of comparable sales can be supplied, and a review of the appraisal can be requested from the underwriter. A second appraisal can also be requested. Sometimes the appraiser who valued the property is not familiar with the area. In that case, the buyer has every right to contact the underwriter (preferably in writing) and demand that a local appraiser be used.

WHEN TO MAKE A PRICE ADJUSTMENT

How do you know when and if you should adjust the price of your home if it hasn't yet sold? The answer to that question is somewhat situational and depends on your goals and your local market. We do have some broad guidelines that you can use to help determine if now is the right time to reduce the price of your home.

If your home has been on the market for 30 days and has had few showings or no offers, it may be time to reduce the asking price. In some markets, 30 days is too long to wait. If homes in your area normally sell within the first 2 weeks, you'll want to adjust the price much sooner.

When market conditions change, you may need to consider adjusting the price downward. If a home just like yours comes on the market and is priced 10% below your asking price, you must address this new competition. You can either find a concrete way to show that your home is worth the extra 10% or reduce the price if you want to stay competitive on price.

Take your goals and needs into consideration. If you need a quick sale to meet financial obligations or for personal reasons, you may make the adjustment sooner than someone who has no constraints. But waiting too long can result in an even lower sale price because buyers begin to think something is wrong with the home. Buyers may smell a deal, thinking you must be getting anxious to sell.

You and your Realtor should talk about your plan for making a price adjustment at the time you list the home. You don't want to feel pressured to decide on the spur of the moment. It's much better to plan ahead.

KEY TAKE-AWAYS

- Your home is entering a competition

- The value that matters in the value in the eyes of the buyer

- Careful market analysis is vital

- It's unintuitive, but an asking price that is too high can result in a lower sale price

CONDITION AND FEATURES

And How They Impact Price

Husband to wife: "Ask the Realtor if we can list the litter box as a third bathroom." – Randy Glasbergen / glasbergen.com

I f a home has incredible features but also has a host of small glitches such as a broken window, burned out light bulbs or worn and dirty carpeting in the master bedroom, the best features of the home may be overshadowed by these annoying little distractions. When a home does not have the same level of features as other, similar homes in the same area, should you hire a contractor to do the upgrades? If you do upgrade your kitchen, will you make your investment back at the closing table? What upgrades are most likely to add value to your home, and which ones would more readily grab a buyer's interest?

David and Victoria Ranck

THE RELATIONSHIP BETWEEN CONDITION AND PRICE

If you want to command a prestige price for your home, it must be in tip-top shape. The smallest of details matter. If a home has great features but isn't in the greatest condition, the market value will decrease in the eyes of a buyer. Even simple things like old paint can drastically lower the perceived value of a home. Painting is not an expensive project, and many buyers will be turned off by the appearance of a home with worn or outdated paint. That uniquely painted accent wall – you know the neon purple wall in the dining room - you might love it but will the average buyer like it or will it turn them off?

Balancing the cost of repairs or improvements with the list price of a home is a delicate matter. Should you put on a new roof? A new roof is a rather expensive upgrade after all. The answer is: it depends. To answer the question, you must determine if the condition of the roof will prevent the home from selling and cause the price to be reduced too much. Even if you price the home lower to allow for the installation of a new roof, buyers may walk away because they just don't want to deal with the headache of a construction project that large.

The bottom line is that the better condition your home is in, the higher price you can expect. In the following chart we see that the closer a home's condition is to "pristine" (toward the left), the higher price point. If the home is in poor condition, the price point is much lower.

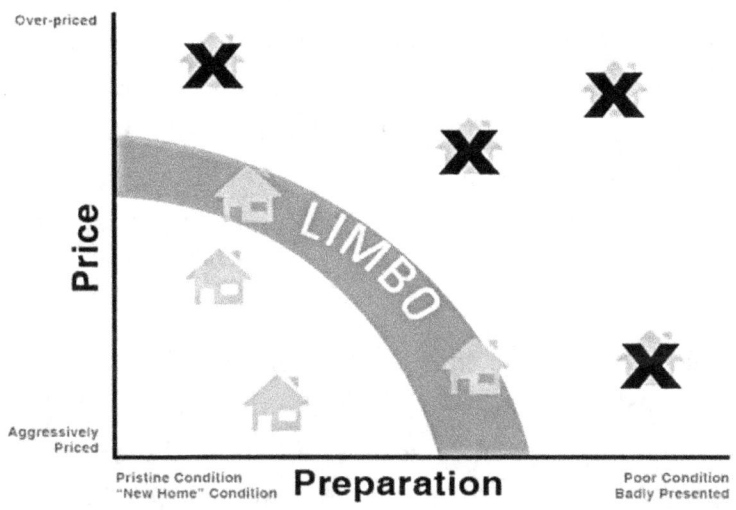

The homes with the X's through them are priced too high and are in too poor of a condition to sell. The 2 homes on the grey curved area are "pushing the envelope" and may not sell quickly or without at least a small price reduction. Of course, the alternative to a price reduction is to improve the condition of the home. This doesn't necessarily mean taking on a large, expensive project. It could mean cleaning up the yard or repainting the exterior. Fixing poor condition can be something as involved as replacing an old, failing roof or as simple as weeding an untended garden.

David and Victoria Ranck

CASE STUDY #3
HE ALMOST LEFT $40,000 ON THE TABLE

A home remodeler had purchased a foreclosed home in a great neighborhood. The area was full of mature trees, shining lakes and it was near a golf course. He really did an exceptional job remodeling the home and added exceptional upgrades to every room. By the time he was done, the home looked like something out of a magazine. Since we have sold many homes in the area, we watched his progress with interest.

He mentioned to us that he was going to list the home for $290,000. At that asking price the home would probably have sold for about $275,000. Because we know the area well and were aware of recent sales, we strongly felt that he could ask quite a bit more for the home. We explained our reasoning to him and described several nearby homes that had recently sold for over $300,000. We compared his home feature by feature to the ones that sold for the higher prices and with homes that sold for less.

In the end he took our advice and listed the home for $319,000. And when we put the word out, an agent brought a buyer that loved the home so much that they paid full asking price immediately! The home was under contract before the listing was able to be uploaded to the MLS. The bottom line: the home sold for about $40,000 more than it would have at the seller's original list price.

REAL ESTATE IS HYPER-LOCAL

Ok, we've talked about things that can cause the perceived value of a home to be reduced in the eyes of a buyer and we've seen how setting a price that is too high can surprisingly result in a lower sale price. Let's turn things on their head and see what you can do so your home commands a higher price than similar homes in the same neighborhood.

Keep in mind that Real Estate is hyper-local. Homes in different neighborhoods within a town will have differing factors that affect the selling price. Even within a single community, variations can exist from street to street. Let's say that the homes on one street in a gated community are larger, have a more elegant interior design and have crown molding in every room as standard. On another street, the homes aren't as large, don't have some of the upscale architectural features and don't commonly have crown molding.

If a home on the first street does not have crown molding, it will almost certainly have a negative effect on the sale price. Adding crown molding to this home won't add value above the competing homes on the street. It will add parity with them. On the second street, adding crown molding to the home will make it stand out above the other homes and may contribute in providing an impetus to raise the price above the neighboring homes. That's an example of what hyper-local means.

PROJECTS LIKELY TO ADD VALUE TO A HOME

The following is a list of interior projects / upgrades that are likely to add value to your home. This list is taken from the "2017 Remodeling Impact Report" published by the National Association of Realtors (Remodeling Impact Report, 2017). This report contains data that reflects the national averages. Keep this in mind as you review the data.

Projects that are likely to add value to the home for resale (highest to lowest):

1. Complete Kitchen Renovation
2. Kitchen Upgrade
3. Bathroom Renovation
4. Add New Bathroom
5. New Master Suite / Owners' Suite
6. New Wood Flooring
7. HVAC Replacement
8. Hardwood Flooring Refinish
9. Basement Conversion to Living Area
10. Attic Conversion to Living Area
11. Closet Renovation
12. Insulation Upgrade

The list above shows the projects that are likely to allow the home to command a higher price. It doesn't indicate that you will recoup all the costs of the projects! The next list shows what upgrades most appeal to buyers. The distinction may seem subtle at first. This list describes order of upgrades that will get a buyer's attention.

David and Victoria Ranck

Projects that most appeal to buyers (highest to lowest):

1. Complete Kitchen Renovation
2. Kitchen Upgrade
3. Bathroom Renovation
4. New Wood Flooring
5. Add New Bathroom
6. Hardwood Flooring Refinish
7. New Master Suite / Owners' Suite
8. HVAC Replacement
9. Basement Conversion to Living Area
10. Closet Renovation
11. Insulation Upgrade
12. Attic Conversion to Living Area

There are subtle differences in the order. For example, New Wood Flooring is in fourth place in the appeal to buyers. When it comes to adding value to a home a New Wood Floor comes in sixth place. What can we learn from this? One improvement may not add as much value to a home as another, but it may make the home easier to sell. In fact, some improvements add absolutely no value to the home, but they may be extremely important to do because they will make the home much easier to sell.

For exterior projects, here is the ranked list of projects most likely to add value from highest to lowest:

1. New Roofing
2. New Vinyl Windows
3. New Garage Door
4. New Vinyl Siding
5. New Wood Windows
6. New Steel Front Door
7. New Fiber-Cement Siding
8. New Fiberglass Front Door

And here is the list of the exterior projects most desired by buyers ranked from highest to lowest:

1. New Roofing
2. New Vinyl Windows
3. New Garage Door
4. New Vinyl Siding
5. New Steel Front Door
6. New Wood Windows
7. New Fiberglass Front Door
8. New Fiber-Cement Siding

As with the interior projects, there are subtle differences in the order. Now let's see how much of a return on investment we might receive on these projects.

RETURN ON INVESTMENT (ROI)

Using the same report from the National Association of Realtors (Remodeling Impact Report, 2017), let's look at the Return on Investment that can be expected from some of these upgrades. ROI is a calculation of how much money you can expect to get back on any renovation when you sell your home.

ROI is simple to calculate. Let's say you decide to add beautiful wood flooring to your home. The total charges by the contractor for materials and labor is $4,500. The estimated cost recovery when you sell your home is $5,000. Subtracting the amount paid from the amount recovered gives us a total of $500. If we divide the $500 gain by the original cost of $4,500, and express it as a percentage, we gained 11% on our investment for an ROI of 111%.

I'll review each upgrade listed above in turn and provide the NAR Remodeler's cost estimate, the Realtor's estimated cost recovery and the ROI. I'll also provide Realtor's suggestions to homeowners for each upgrade.

INTERIOR PROJECTS

New Master Suite
    Estimated cost: $125,000
    Estimated Recovery: $65,000
    ROI: 52%.

Only 4% of Realtors suggested that sellers perform this upgrade before selling their home. Only 1% said this project recently helped to close a deal.

Kitchen Upgrade
    Estimated cost: $35,000
    Estimated Recovery: $20,000
    ROI: 57%.

54% of Realtors suggested that sellers perform this upgrade before selling their home. 23% said this project recently helped to close a deal.

Complete Kitchen Renovation
    Estimated cost: $65,000
    Estimated Recovery: $40,000
    ROI: 62%.

David and Victoria Ranck

18% of Realtors suggested that sellers perform this upgrade before selling their home. 14% said this project recently helped to close a deal.

Bathroom Renovation
Estimated cost: $30,000
Estimated Recovery: $15,000
ROI: 50%.

54% of Realtors suggested that sellers perform this upgrade before selling their home. Only 6% said this project recently helped to close a deal.

Add a New Bathroom
Estimated cost: $59,000
Estimated Recovery: $29,750
ROI: 50%.

7% of Realtors suggested that sellers perform this upgrade before selling their home. Only 1% said this project recently helped to close a deal.

Attic Conversion to Living Area
Estimated cost: $75,000
Estimated Recovery: $40,000
ROI: 53%.

Only 2% of Realtors suggested that sellers perform this

upgrade before selling their home. No Realtors said this project recently helped to close a deal.

Insulation Upgrade
Estimated cost: $2,100
Estimated Recovery: $1,600
ROI: 76%.

5% of Realtors suggested that sellers perform this upgrade before selling their home. Only 1% said this project recently helped to close a deal.

Closet Renovation
Estimated cost: $3,750
Estimated Recovery: $2,000
ROI: 53%.

5% of Realtors suggested that sellers perform this upgrade before selling their home. No Realtors said this project recently helped to close a deal.

New Wood Flooring
Estimated cost: $5,500
Estimated Recovery: $5,000
ROI: 91%.

21% of Realtors suggested that sellers perform this upgrade before selling their home. 7% said this project recently helped to close a deal.

David and Victoria Ranck

Wood Floor Refinishing

    Estimated cost: $3,000

    Estimated Recovery: $3,000

    ROI: 100%.

37% of Realtors suggested that sellers perform this upgrade before selling their home. 6% said this project recently helped to close a deal.

HVAC Replacement

    Estimated cost: $7,475

    Estimated Recovery: $5,000

    ROI: 67%.

23% of Realtors suggested that sellers perform this upgrade before selling their home. 6% said this project recently helped to close a deal.

EXTERIOR PROJECTS

New Steel Front Door
> Estimated cost: $2,000
> Estimated Recovery: $1,500
> ROI: 75%.

> 7% of Realtors suggested that sellers perform this upgrade before selling their home. Only 1% said this project recently helped to close a deal.

New Fiberglass Front Door
> Estimated cost: $2,700
> Estimated Recovery: $1,800
> ROI: 67%.

> 6% of Realtors suggested that sellers perform this upgrade before selling their home. Only 1% said this project recently helped to close a deal.

New Garage Door
> Estimated cost: $2,300
> Estimated Recovery: $2,000
> ROI: 87%.

> 24% of Realtors suggested that sellers perform this

upgrade before selling their home. Only 1% said this project recently helped to close a deal.

New Vinyl Siding
Estimated cost: $13,350
Estimated Recovery: $10,000
ROI: 75%.

6% of Realtors suggested that sellers perform this upgrade before selling their home. Only 1% said this project recently helped to close a deal.

New Fiber-Cement Siding
Estimated cost: $18,000
Estimated Recovery: $15,000
ROI: 83%.

Just 3% of Realtors suggested that sellers perform this upgrade before selling their home. Only 1% said this project recently helped to close a deal.

New Roofing
Estimated cost: $7,500
Estimated Recovery: $8,150
ROI: 109%.

45% of Realtors suggested that sellers perform this upgrade before selling their home. 32% said this project recently helped to close a deal. This one is a good bet!

New Vinyl Windows

Estimated cost: $18,975

Estimated Recovery: $15,000

ROI: 79%.

21% of Realtors suggested that sellers perform this upgrade before selling their home. 8% said this project recently helped to close a deal.

New Wood Windows

Estimated cost: $35,000

Estimated Recovery: $20,000

ROI: 57%.

4% of Realtors suggested that sellers perform this upgrade before selling their home. Only 1% said this project recently helped to close a deal.

Most of the upgrades listed above do not have an ROI equal to or greater than the cost. Sometimes a homeowner calculates the value of his or her home by adding up what the contractors were paid to perform all the changes made to the home over the last several years. It would be nice if this were a valid way to evaluate the price of a home, but as you can see, things don't work that way. The only value that matters is the Value in the Eyes of the Buyer. It may be hard to swallow, but how much we paid for our upgrades doesn't even factor into the equation when we are putting a value on our home. But remember...

Real Estate is hyper-local.

LOCAL MARKET UPGRADES AND ROI

In a local market, certain upgrades will add more value than the national average would indicate, and some improvements will add less value than the national average. ROI will differ too because material and labor costs vary from region to region. The figures below were taken from the "Remodeling 2018 Cost vs. Value Report" published by Remodeling Magazine (Remodeling 2018 Cost vs. Value Report, 2018). They are specific to the Sarasota, Florida area. You can find additional data on Sarasota and data for other areas at www.costvsvalue.com.

New Roofing
National Averages
Cost: $20,939

Recovery: $14,320

ROI: 68.4%

Sarasota
Cost: $18,857

Recovery: $16,519

ROI: 82.8%

Minor Kitchen Remodel (Midrange)
National Averages
Cost: $ 63,829

Recovery: $ 37,637

ROI: 59.0%

Sarasota
Cost: $ 60,052

Recovery: $ 36,027

ROI: 60.0%

Major Kitchen Remodel (Midrange)
National Averages
Cost: $ 21,198

Recovery: $ 17,193

ROI: 81.1%

Sarasota

Cost: $ 20,103
Recovery: $ 17,002
ROI: 84.6%

Bathroom Remodel (Midrange)
National Averages
Cost: $ 19,134
Recovery: $ 13,422
ROI: 70.1%

Sarasota
Cost: $ 17,247
Recovery: $ 14,333
ROI: 83.1%

Garage Door Replacement
National Averages
Cost: $ 3,470
Recovery: $ 3,411
ROI: 98.3%

Sarasota
Cost: $ 3,462
Recovery: $ 4,023
ROI: 116.2%

As we can see, the local data can vary considerably from the national data. There is one common element that is consistent across geographic boundaries: Most upgrade projects do not result in a 100% or greater ROI. *The average ROI is less than 66%.* Keep that fact in mind when you are choosing whether to undertake an upgrade. Of course, ROI is not the only reason for upgrading your kitchen and bath! You should get enjoyment out of your home and if putting in a chef-class kitchen will make you happy, then by all means do it! Realize though that you may not recoup all the costs of the kitchen when you sell your home. Be OK with that. ROI isn't everything and we shouldn't live our lives exclusively by the numbers. At some point we should do things because we enjoy them or do them to bless someone special in our lives.

Localized data source:
© 2018 Hanley Wood Media Inc.
Complete data from the Remodeling 2018 Cost vs. Value Report can be downloaded free at www.costvsvalue.com.

KEY TAKE-AWAYS

- The condition of a home has a significant impact on the sales price and even on your ability to sell the home

- Real Estate is hyper-local. When considering upgrades, it is important to understand the local market, even down to the level of a single street within a community

- Return on Investment or ROI shows what percentage of the cost of an upgrade may be recouped when the home sells

- Most upgrades do not have positive ROI so choose your projects wisely – the average remodeling project recoups less than two thirds of its cost when the home sells

PRESENTATION

Getting Ready for the Big Game

"Houses are like people – some you like and some you don't like – and once in a while there is one you love." — L.M. Montgomery, Emily Climbs

Take a deep breath. The ball has been moved a long way down the field. You've done your research and now you have a good idea how your home stacks up against the competition. You've decided what upgrades you are going do or not do and you have decided on a fair market price for your home. Now let's find out what it will take for everyone else to realize just how great your home is. You'll discover how to dress it up and get it ready for the ball.

We all know the adage "Don't judge a book by its cover". If we are honest, that's exactly how everyone judges a book. When we put our house on the market, we have exactly one chance to make a great first impression with each buyer. We must take full advantage of this fleeting opportunity to get them excited about their new home. The house may have "good bones" but if buyers can't see past the taste-specific décor or the unkempt front yard, the home's unique features won't matter.

Always remember – in today's market, homebuyers can afford to be choosy. Buyers are looking for the best value for the price, so your home needs to be in the best condition possible. When Victoria and I preview a home before it's listed, we offer the owners advice on simple changes that go a long way to helping buyers to see themselves having a wonderful life in their new home. In this section we'll review the most effective tips and tricks that will help to get buyers excited about YOUR home.

FIRST IMPRESSIONS MATTER

There's a commercial that began playing on TV a while ago and I chuckle every time I see it. A couple meets at a restaurant and sits down at a table. I get the idea that that they have been dating online and this is their first face-to-face meet up. The guy says to the girl, "You look great!". She smiles and says to him, "You look, uh, quite – comfortable...". He grins awkwardly because he realizes that the neckline of his t-shirt is all stretched out and looks weird.

We only have one shot at making a first impression and having a buyer view your home is a bit like online dating. The relationship starts out online, so the photos and description must pique their interest enough so that they'll want to meet for a first date. We want them to be excited to see your home in person. When they come in for a showing, we want them to fall in love at first sight. If a buyer's first impression is negative, it can be exceedingly difficult to reverse it later. Will your home meet their expectations, or will they pass on it and move on?

To ensure their first impression is a good one, you must understand how buyers will look at your home. It can be difficult, but separate yourself from your emotional attachment to your home. Try to look at it as if you are seeing it for the first time. Put yourself in the shoes of a buyer walking from the curb to your front door. What do they see? Is there anything that would distract them from a good impression? As you walk through the front door, what is the first thing that grabs your attention, positive or negative? Walk through your entire home and make notes about your positive and negative impressions. I know it isn't easy but try to be objective.

Because it is hard to distance yourself from the home that you've lived in and enjoyed for many years, a good Realtor will provide you with an objective viewpoint. We'll often notice things that the owners miss – both good and bad. Sometimes the things about a home that make a super positive impression on us are not even on the owner's radar. They've lived there so long they take for granted the things that make their home special that we see.

One especially important and often ignored first impression is the presence of odors in your home. If you have pets, especially cats, you must make certain any smells are completely eliminated. Pets aren't the only source of odors. I had one buyer notice an off-putting smell at one of our open houses. I had been in the home many times and had never smelled anything unpleasant. I had her show me where the odor was the strongest and I finally noticed it too. I traced it down to the plant beds in the lanai. To me the smell was very subtle but to her it was strong enough that she was not interested in the home.

Like the couple in the TV commercial, you start your relationship with the buyer online. We'll go over photography in the next section but hiring a pro is only one part of the task. First the home must be made ready for the photos. Your home looks different in person than it does in photos. You know the old saying that the camera puts on 10 pounds? In a home, the camera accentuates things like colors, clutter and a lack of lighting.

LESS IS MORE

Most of us are collectors. Over the years that we've lived in our homes, we've acquired lots of Stuff. We put our stuff throughout our home because *we* enjoy it and because we find it useful. We have lots of plants scattered throughout our home or we have bookshelves full of the novels we've read over the last 15 years. We like all our things out where we can see them and where we can readily get to them. There is another word for all this stuff: Clutter.

Decluttering is one of the most important steps in getting your home ready for the camera and for buyers. It can be difficult to do because you must be 100% objective and ruthless in removing items that don't appeal to a wide audience. A client of ours told her friend just how hard it was for her as we walked through her home and recommended things she should remove. It was painful. But a week after it was done, she called her friend and told her "I should have had Vicky come over years ago!".

You want your home to attract the highest number of buyers and that means filtering items down to the basics that have the widest appeal. Victoria calls this process "Editing". Think of your home as a hotel room. How cluttered is a room in an upscale hotel? It isn't cluttered at all, but it is still quite attractive. There are no knickknacks, nothing without a purpose. Your home should look more like a hotel room than it probably does today. You want your home to feel comfortable and inviting, and you want buyers to concentrate on your home's unique features. Anything that may distract buyers must be removed and stored away out of sight.

You've heard the saying "The camera puts on 10 pounds". The camera also accentuates busy-ness and clutter in a home's décor. Buy a home decorating magazine and study the photos or watch a show about rehabbing a home on TV. Note how uncluttered the rooms are. Everything has a place, and everything is in its place. Less is more when it comes to preparing your home's décor for sale.

Renting a storage space may be the best investment you can make in selling your home. Spending $50 - $100 a month on a storage space could net you $5000 or more on the sale of your home. Now that you've removed the clutter, give your home a deep cleaning.

A clean home gives buyers the impression that the home has been well cared for. By clean I mean spotlessly clean from top to bottom. This includes cleaning ceiling fan blades and AC grills, dusting the tops of doorways and baseboards (a favorite habitat of dust bunnies!). There should not be a single surface in your home that is left untouched. Wash the windows – especially if one of your home's features is a great view. Have your carpets cleaned and make tile and hardwood floors shine. Consider hiring a professional cleaning crew to spruce up your home. They can save you a lot of time and effort. Have them come and clean periodically while your home is on the market.

The kitchen deserves special mention. We use our kitchen every day and we may be used to letting dishes pile up in the sink throughout the day. The kitchen counters tend to accumulate a lot of clutter. Get in the habit of immediately putting dishes into the dishwasher and wiping down the counters after every meal so your home is always ready to show. Wipe fingerprints off stainless appliances every day. Keep the stove spotless. If you have a ceramic surface electric stove, get a special cleaning solution and remove all the stains and burned on food. With the right cleaner and a razor blade, you can make almost any ceramic surface stove look brand new. One more tip: clean your oven. Buyers will open the oven door!

If you want to see some samples of how your home definitely should NOT look when you put it up for sale, check out the site Ugly House Photos 2.0 at this link: https://moreuglyhousephotos.tumblr.com/. Some the homes there are in terrible condition, but many are just very cluttered, unkempt or in serious need of a good cleaning.

THROUGH THE EYES OF A BUYER

It is important to have someone who has an objective viewpoint help you with this next task. When it's our home, we can be too attached to our favorite things and we might be reluctant to make the changes that will help the home appeal to the highest number of buyers. When Victoria helps a homeowner edit their home in preparation to putting it on the market, she walks through every room and views it through the eyes of a buyer. She has the experience to see things the way a buyer does and since she is not emotionally attached to the home, she can be objective about what should stay and what should go. Keep the end in mind – you want to sell your home for the most money in the shortest amount of time. Don't let sentimental attachments to things interfere with your ultimate goal.

Here's what I want you to do: Get in your car and drive away from your home. Take a pad and pen with you. Maybe go have lunch. Then drive back and park in front of your home, where buyers might park when coming to an open house or a showing. Get out of your car and look at the front of your home as if you are seeing it for the first time. Compare it with other homes on the street. Walk up the path to your front door and into the entryway. Write down the good things that you see and feel, and the less than good. Be as objective as you can be. Go through your home room by room, taking notes along the way.

You've likely heard the phrase "beauty is in the eye of the beholder." In other words, the person observing something gets to decide its worth – and what I think is beautiful and what you find beautiful may differ wildly! – (Sales Enablement Is In The Eye Of The Buyer, 2018)

Do your best to put yourself in the shoes of a buyer. If you can, take someone with you that will speak bluntly with you and that will tell you what you need to hear, not what you want to hear. This is where a good, a really good Realtor can be invaluable. He or she is invested in your success and will help you see things through another set of eyes – experienced, objective eyes.

David and Victoria Ranck

I may love the bright green accent wall in my home office, but will a potential buyer love it too? Or will it become an obstacle that prevents them from envisioning themselves living in the home? And Yes – I do have a bright green wall in my home office! It will also be painted a neutral color before we have photos taken when we list our house for sale.

You may have a great collection of Russian dolls, movie posters or ceramic birds. As much as you love them, buyers don't want to see them. Knickknacks on shelves and tables should be stored away. I know this can be hard to do. You have these things because you love them, and you like to show them to visitors. But very individualistic items can prevent a buyer from envisioning your home as their home.

You must look for anything in your home that is "Taste-specific". My green wall is specific to my taste. Victoria would never have chosen that color. It doesn't mean I have bad taste, just that in this instance my taste probably appeals to a narrow audience. That's OK unless my goal is to attract as many buyers as possible and to sell my home quickly and at a good price.

What do you do if there is something about your home that might not have mass appeal but is something you can't easily change? Perhaps your home has floor-to-ceiling shelving in the living room or a built-in entertainment center. Find a way to make it a selling feature. Don't try to hide it. Perhaps you could place attractive art pieces on the shelves along with

LED lighted candles to provide a soft, warm look. Be creative and think outside of the box. Find a way to make it work for you instead of against you.

You may have heard that you should de-personalize your home when you get it ready to sell. Conventional wisdom says that you should remove all family photos from your home to enable buyers to visualize the home as their own. I absolutely agree, if you have an entire wall of family photos or have multitudes of these photos everywhere in your home, you'll want to remove most of them. Some recent articles I've read indicate that having *a few* family photos may be OK and can help to humanize your home. When in doubt though, hide them away.

STAGING

Staging a home involves carefully choosing furniture and accessories and placing them in a way that brings out the best in the home. Staging is often used when a home is unoccupied and completely empty of furniture. The principles apply to all homes, even if furniture is present. You probably don't need to get rid of all your furniture, just continue the "editing" process we spoke of earlier. If you have bulky furniture that overcrowds a room, consider replacing it with rented items more suitable for the space.

"I see many home sellers confuse staging with decorating and consequently resisting the process and the recommendations of the staging professional. But the reality is that the moment you commit to marketing your home for sale, you need to commit to transforming your home into a place that potential buyers can easily picture as their home. This means that you need to be prepared to emotionally detach." – Kris Berg (Sellers: The Benefits of Staging Your Home, p. 2018)

Don't confuse staging with decorating. Decorating is what we do to make our home our own. We stage a home to help buyers envision the home as their own. The goal of staging is to give your home a voice that speaks clearly to buyers and Realtors. The message you want to convey is: "You would love living in this home!". Staging is the language that communicates that message loudly and clearly. Most importantly it brings the message home using emotion, not just logic. Logic makes us think but emotion leads us to act.

Does staging a home really matter? Will it make a difference in a home's time on market and sale price? The National Association of Realtors published their findings on the impact of staging on home sales in the 2017 Profile of Home Staging by (Profile of Home Staging, 2017).

David and Victoria Ranck

In this report:

- 49% of buyer's agents (Realtors representing the buyer, not the listing agent) said that staging influenced most buyer's view of the home
- 77% of buyer's agents said staging a home made it easier for a buyer to visualize the property as a future home
- Staging the living room for buyers was found to be most important (55%), followed by staging the master bedroom (51%), and staging the kitchen (41%)
- 39% of sellers' agents stated that staging a home greatly decreases the amount of time the home is on the market
- Buyers were more willing to walk through a home they saw online (40%), and buyers' agents identified that staging would positively impact the home value if the home was decorated to a buyer's taste (38%)

How did staging affect the sale price according to the listing agent?

- 29% said the price increased from 1% to 5%
- 21% said the price increased from 6% to 10%
- 5% said the price increased from 11% to 15%
- 3% said the price increased from 16% to 20%
- 14% said staging had no impact on price
- 27% were unsure

How much does it cost to have a home professionally staged? The cost depends on how many rooms are staged, the size of the rooms and the type of furnishings used. Upscale homes will generally cost more to stage. An average home here in southwest Florida can cost $1600 - $1800 to stage 3 rooms. After the first month, the cost goes down to perhaps $500 per month.

Are the benefits of professional staging worth the cost? Using the data above and the expected sale price of the home, you can get a good idea of what you may expect. If you have about a 30% chance of getting from 6% to 20% more for your home and you're selling price is $350,000, it looks like a good deal. But keep in mind that sales price is not the only reason to stage your home. 39% of seller's agents said that staging greatly reduced the time on market. You probably have carrying costs – taxes, HOA fees, a mortgage payment, insurance, utilities, etc. Factor those costs into your decision.

There are alternatives to professional staging. One we will discuss in the section on marketing: Virtual Staging. Another option is to rent furniture. Renting furniture may cost less than hiring a professional stager, but you lose their expertise. If you are a great decorator or know someone who is, this may be a reasonable replacement for a pro. If your home is not empty, then accenting your home by bringing in a few new pieces may do the trick. Carefully stage bathrooms, the kitchen and the master bedroom. See our checklist below for some ideas.

Finally remember that Real Estate is Hyper-Local! The results of staging your home may depend on your location, the local market conditions and the competition. If all the other homes in your area are staged, your home will need to be professionally staged just to keep up. On the other hand, professional staging may be a great way to get a leg up on your competition.

HOME PREPARATION CHECKLIST

Here's a checklist you can use to prepare your home for sale:

Entrance
- ✓ Paint the front door
- ✓ Replace worn hardware
- ✓ Stage the front porch
- ✓ Sweep away cobwebs in entryway
- ✓ Touch up paint on trim
- ✓ Remove any insect nests
- ✓ Get a new welcome mat
- ✓ Don't let shoes pile up inside the front door

General
- ✓ Clean the home from top to bottom
- ✓ Wash the windows
- ✓ Declutter / "edit"
- ✓ Paint walls in neutral colors
- ✓ Repaint trim as needed
- ✓ Use "Magic Erasers" to remove scuffs from walls
- ✓ Make floors shine
- ✓ Have carpets cleaned
- ✓ Replace burned-out lightbulbs
- ✓ Fix minor issues like leaky faucets or broken glass
- ✓ Find and remove the source of unpleasant smells
- ✓ Have gutters cleaned and roof swept of debris

- ✓ Pressure wash tile roof if needed

Kitchen and Bath
- ✓ Clean out the oven and outdoor grill
- ✓ Clean out the refrigerator and remove all magnets, etc.
- ✓ Organize the kitchen – remove counter top appliances
- ✓ Keep the kitchen clean and the sink free of dishes
- ✓ Organize the bathrooms
- ✓ Remove soap dispensers, toothbrushes, hairbrushes, razors, etc. from counters and hide in drawers or cabinets
- ✓ Keep attractive clean towels neatly hung on towel bars

Bedrooms
- ✓ Keep beds made
- ✓ Remove personal grooming products
- ✓ Organize your closets – if over-stuffed, remove items you don't need
- ✓ If you've converted 2 of 3 bedrooms into offices or storage, convert at least one of them back to a bedroom
- ✓ Use inflatable beds with sheets, duvet and pillows if a bedroom is empty

Living Room / Dining Room
- ✓ Clean the furniture

- ✓ Hide magazine racks
- ✓ Keep coffee tables clear except for decorative items
- ✓ Hide TV / Stereo wiring
- ✓ Hide an old dining room table with a table cloth
- ✓ Keep dining room table free of homework, papers, etc.

Outdoor Spaces
- ✓ Clean up the garden
- ✓ Add new mulch
- ✓ Keep grass cut
- ✓ Trim hedges and bushes
- ✓ Spruce up landscaping
- ✓ Clean patio furniture
- ✓ Clean lanai screens
- ✓ Keep pool clean
- ✓ Remove toys and clutter from around the pool
- ✓ Keep driveway swept
- ✓ Pressure wash driveway and walkways
- ✓ Clean out and organize the garage

Wow. That seems like a lot of things to do! Keep the 80/20 rule in mind – tackle the most important items first. If you're unsure of where to start, get some advice. Ask your Realtor for his or her thoughts.

You've worked hard getting your home ready for sale. Now it's time to attract buyers and get them to come in for an in-person tour.

KEY TAKE-AWAYS

- Buyers can afford to be choosy - make your home attractive to the widest possible audience

- A buyer's first impressions are extremely important. It's hard to reverse negative first impressions.

- Less is more - decluttering your home is fundamental

- Clean your home from top to bottom

- See your home through the eyes of a buyer, be objective

- Stage and/or "edit" your home to appeal to most buyers

- Go through the Home Preparation Checklist before selling your home

PART THREE:
NEW TOOLS FOR
A NEW MARKET

How to Gain an Unfair Advantage
Over the Competition

The leverage and influence social media gives
citizens are rapidly spreading into the
business world. - Simon Mainwaring

Your home has been staged and is ready for the world to see. You've carefully chosen a listing price that meets your goals and fits the marketplace. Lightbulbs have been replaced, the floors shine, and you have made arrangements for Fido and Fluffy when buyers come for a showing.

The previous chapters provide the essential foundation to market your home using today's technology. Technology alone won't sell your home. It must be wisely and artfully implemented. A Facebook advertisement may reach thousands of potential buyers but if the message and the images are not compelling, it won't be effective. No one will click through to view your home's details and schedule a showing. Social Media marketing must be supported by a great Lifestyle Narrative, professional photos, and traditional marketing techniques such as mailings and phone calls.

Now is the time to implement the Marketing Plan. The keyword is "Plan". Plan the Work and Work the Plan.

USE TECHNOLOGY TO MEET BUYERS WHERE THEY ARE

Marketing Your Home in Today's Tech-enabled World

Smart phones and social media expand our universe. We can connect with others or collect information easier and faster than ever.
- Daniel Goleman

W e know that buyers invariably start their search for a new home on the Internet, so marketing should leverage online resources as much as possible. With every home for sale listed on the Internet, there is a lot of noise. As I'm writing this, there are almost 10,000 homes currently for sale in Sarasota and Manatee counties in

Florida. Every one of those homes is on the Internet and the big syndicated sites. In the last 4 weeks, a little over 1300 homes have sold. How can your home stand out in the middle of all this noise and be one of the homes that sell?

You must go where the buyers are and they are on Social Media like Facebook, YouTube and Pinterest. Social Media and the Internet are where you meet most buyers, so your home must look its best on the web. To truly take advantage of the power of these technologies they must also be combined with more traditional strategies like open houses and direct mail.

Marketing is the sum of all the activities you take to get your home sold. It starts with reaching buyers online and ends with how your home shows when they schedule a showing and walk through your home. The important take-away is that Everything is marketing. Don't skip the basics we talked about earlier. And remember that the biggest marketing tool you have at hand is the proper pricing of your home.

In this chapter we'll discuss how you can leverage technology to make your home stand out among the online crowd. We'll discuss:
- Prerequisites to putting your home online
- Facebook and Instagram
- YouTube
- Pinterest

- Tried and true techniques that still work today
- Creating a marketing plan for your home

Start Off on the Right Foot

You only have one chance to make a first impression with buyers. Many agents stumble on this step and cost their sellers real money when buyers don't value the home enough to make solid offers. How can you avoid this misstep? Much of the property marketing campaign rests on the buyer's ability to find your property online... and when found that it has the right information. Don't skip the foundational steps and not hire a Professional Photographer or take the time to write a compelling Lifestyle Narrative.

THE LIFESTYLE NARRATIVE

Logic makes us Think but Emotion makes us Act.

As a lifelong observer of human behavior, particularly in the area of business, a large percentage of the time, emotion wins this ever-going arm wrestle when it comes to purchasing a new car, choosing an item at the supermarket, signing for a new home, or choosing a woman to wed. - Michael Levine (Levine, 2012)

Consider these excerpts from real-world listings:

"Ready to move in, remodeled, great location, lanai with a golf course view. Two story with no carpet. Large ceramic tile downstairs and wood laminate upstairs. Large indoor laundry room"

"Charming 2 bedroom 1 bathroom home ... with large living room"

"This is a good opportunity for a large 4 bedroom, 3 bath, pool home with 2961 square feet ... Interior features include a large kitchen, separate dining room, living room, and family room with tray ceiling"

"New paint and flooring throughout, and bathroom tile in the lower bath in this open plan unit. The entrance is a large screened-in deck and patio, that has been freshly painted, and overlooks a wooded area"

"Fully updated with tile floors, new kitchen, and bathrooms. Open living room with lots of natural light. Spacious dining room opens up to the kitchen area"

Are these descriptions addressing the buyer's logic or emotions? While some of the terms used may trigger some emotional response, by and large the listing agents are using more pragmatic terminology that at least to me, is boring and flat. Unfortunately, even the full descriptions of these listings were not much longer or more interesting. I didn't spend hours combing the MLS trying to find these examples - they were returned in the first 2 pages of my search results. Sigh.

Now read through this marketing narrative:

"This move in ready, immaculate Greenbrook home feels like your own private resort. High ceilings, crown molding and an elegant dining room flanked by 10' columns complete its charm. Family and friends will gather around the saltwater pool with its 2 covered lanais while you entertain for 2 or 20 in the open kitchen with a chef's island and stainless appliances.

Slide open the patio doors and they completely disappear bringing the outdoors right into the family room. Your friends will gather around the built-in entertainment center on Super Bowl Sunday, dipping chips into salsa while chili simmers on the stove. Guests will never forget their overnight stay in the pool-side bedroom with its own private bath. After a long day, imagine yourself unwinding in the garden tub while your cares melt away. Or when you need your own quiet space, retire to the intimate den to relax and recharge.

Take a sunset walk on the nature area path and watch a great heron as she hunts for her dinner. Ride your bike, run or walk the miles of trails all the way into nearby Summerfield. Just a short walk away, both you and your family will love Adventure Park with its playgrounds, dog park, roller hockey rink and volley ball court. Host a grand get-together for friends under the covered pavilion and pick teams for an evening game in one of the 2 soccer fields.

Your home will be both your private oasis and a place your friends and family will enjoy with you."

What part of the brain does this marketing narrative address? In reality, it addresses both the logical and the emotional sides of the brain. Most importantly it draws a mental picture for the buyer who is reading the listing or other material. It showcases the special things about the home and the neighborhood that make it truly exceptional – the home's unique features. We create the Lifestyle Narrative after interviewing the homeowner and finding out what they think is special about their home. After all, who knows your home better than you?

I can't stress the importance of this Lifestyle Narrative too strongly. It forms the basis of all subsequent marketing materials and it shapes our (the listing agents) viewpoint and emotions about the home. When buyers come into an open house, I want to be genuinely excited about the home I am showing them! That excitement rubs off on potential buyers. We reuse this copy many times in mailings, Social Media posts and ads, emails and more so the better it is written, the better those other efforts will perform.

PROFESSIONAL PHOTOGRAPHY

Everyone is a photographer these days because everyone has a smartphone. The trouble is that everyone is not a Professional Photographer. We hire pros for our listings that specialize in Real Estate photography because quality makes a huge difference. Buyers most often search to find a home on the Internet and the first impression they have will be the pictures of the home. If the pictures are "meh", they'll swipe their finger across their phone and move on, never to return.

As we said before, you have mere seconds in which to engage the viewer. Photography is not the place to skimp on your budget. I cringe when I see an $800,000 listing accompanied by smartphone pics that are dark, dreary and that make the home look just terrible. I see this scenario too often.

Fortunately, I also know many Realtors that understand just how important great photos are and like us, pay for a Pro for their clients. Would you put a terrible photo of yourself on a dating website? If you did, would expect many dates? A Pro Real Estate Photographer has the right equipment and the experience to make your home look its best on "film". A good Pro takes a lot of photos, takes them from the correct angles and prepares the room for the best results. After the photographer takes the photos, he or she will perform post-processing to adjust white balance, lighten shadows and color grading. This post-processing ensures the final result portrays the home the way the human eye sees it.

Once the photographer returns the photos, it is time to select the ones that best showcase your home's features. The order in which your Realtor loads the photos into the MLS is important! Remember the 7 second rule. The first few photos must grab the buyer's attention and entice them to read the entire listing. The opening photo usually must be a view of the front of the home to meet MLS rules. You must choose these photos with care and they must look gorgeous. The sky should be interesting and not cloudy and gray. That means the photographer should take them on a sunny and pleasant day. The photographers we use schedule the shoot for the time of day in which the sun is shining on the front of the home. A creative alternative is to shoot these photos at dusk which allows you to feature interior and exterior lighting. If it captures a beautiful sunset behind the home, so much the better.

After the exterior front shot, the next few photos should showcase the best features of the home. Don't feel you need to arrange the photos in order like a walkthrough. If the kitchen is a primary feature, make it the second photo. Follow that by the next most important features and so on. Once your Realtor loads the photos that show the best features into the MLS, he or she can load the remaining shots. I group these photos by room, for example keeping the Master Bedroom and Master Bath together. I also label each photo, so buyers know which room they are viewing.

Encourage the photographer to be creative. A close-in shot of candles on the fireplace mantle or of a wine bottle and glasses on a lanai table can speak volumes to the buyer. Showcase the surrounding area by using landscape photos, or photos of the community amenities. Make sure that the home is the star of the show. When a listing has more photos of the nearby park than of the inside of the home, buyers become suspicious. They may think there is something unattractive about the home that is intentionally being hidden.

Select the best half dozen or so photos and keep them at hand for other marketing collateral. You'll use these photos in Social Media campaigns, direct mail pieces, flyers and email campaigns. One more tip. Make sure the photographer provides you with High Resolution photos, not just images sized for the web. You'll want the hires versions to create print media and a virtual tour (slideshow).

VIDEO CREATION

Video has increased in importance for marketing almost anything online. Video tends to out-perform static images on Social Media sites like Facebook. And get this: the #2 search engine in the world is ... YouTube! If you want buyers to find your home online, you'll want to leverage one or more of the following forms of video.

There are 4 main types of video we use in our marketing plan:

- Virtual Tours
- 3D Interactive Tours
- Walkthrough Videos
- Live Video

Not every home is a good candidate for all four types. Walkthrough videos and 3D tours require the home to show very well. They work best in beautifully decorated or staged homes. If the home has exceptional upgrades, they can also work for empty homes. These videos are also expensive to produce and so are not always appropriate for homes selling below a certain price point.

Virtual Tours

A Virtual Tour in this context is a slideshow of images. The tour may use transitions between images such as a Ken Burns effect or zooming. In our market area, the MLS system creates a default virtual tour from the first five images in the listing. Remember that we said you should carefully choose the first few images? This is another reason why it is important to choose them with care.

The default tours are not always the best-looking tours. I never use them. I have our photographers create a professional tour for each listing. This professional version looks much better than the free version provided by our MLS. There are also websites that will create and host great-looking virtual tours from the listing photos. Every listing of ours gets a professional virtual tour. A great-looking virtual tour helps your home stand out among the competition online.

3D Interactive Tour

A 3D interactive tour uses special cameras and software to create a virtual experience in which buyers can "walk" through the home online. You can view a sample 3D tour here: https://matterport.com/sample-real-estate-listing/. The cost of these tours can be high, and they aren't suitable for all homes. The home must be in pristine condition and staged well for the tour to be effective. You must properly prepare your home because the buyers will be able thoroughly inspect each room. A 3D tour like this can raise the value of a home in the buyer's eyes. Most listings do not have 3D tours, so buyers believe there must something special about the homes that have them. A 3D tour can help differentiate your home from all the others and help it to stand out online.

Walkthrough Videos

A walkthrough video is one in which the agent or owner record themselves going room by room through the home. They comment on the home's features as they go. The equipment used to create these videos varies and if the feeling of the video is casual, a smartphone may be appropriate. I do recommend that the videographer use a stabilizer to keep the images from jumping up and down. I prefer to use a DSLR on a gimbal so that the video quality is higher than a smartphone. Like 3D tours, the home must show well on camera for the video to be effective.

Live Video

Think Facebook Live. This is an impromptu video of the home featuring dialog by the person making the video or by someone who is being interviewed. These videos are not recorded and edited later. They are shot and streamed in real time to a Social Media site. Live video gets more attention on Facebook but since it is live, it is also short-lived. That said, every time I shoot a live video, I get at least a few views. An alternative is shoot video on your phone or DSLR that seems live but is pre-recorded. Using a recorded video on your page may increase its lifetime. Posting a video to Social Media is one way to meet buyers where they are.

Now that your home looks its best, you have a great story to tell in the Lifestyle Narrative and you have professional photos and video, it's time to reveal your home to the world.

FACEBOOK

According to Facebook's own stats, 1.49 billion people used Facebook each day in September 2018. Roughly two-thirds of U.S. adults (68%) now report that they are Facebook users, and roughly three-quarters of those users access Facebook on a daily basis (Social Media Use in 2018). A large number of potential buyers for your home are on Facebook every day. Placing ads, not just posts, on Facebook puts your home in front of all of these people.

Facebook ads work by placing your home in the path of potential buyers as they go about their everyday activities. Think about how billboards work. You drive to work or go to the local coffee shop and you pass a billboard advertising a local business. This happens as part of your normal daily activities. Facebook ads work the same way. Buyer's see your home as they "pass by" your virtual billboard and now they are thinking about your home.

There is an important distinction between Facebook posts and Facebook ads. A post is something you write on your Facebook page and is seen by your network of friends (or your agent's network of friends). It is posted once and over time it falls lower and lower in everyone's feed, unless it is shared. An ad is different. First it is pushed not to your friends but to Facebook users that have shown an interest in buying a home in your area. This group can be narrowly targeted by age, region and interests. Second, it is continually sent out over a period of time, not just once. Third, Facebook ads are not free. It costs money to place ads and they require the user to have a business page. You can and should post about your home on your own page, but you'll need to partner with your Real Estate agent to create Facebook ads.

Facebook ads will use the professional photos and/or video created for your home. The most effective Facebook ads are video ads and carousel ads which display a filmstrip comprised of several pictures. The text of the ad can be drawn from the Lifestyle Narrative and should encourage the user to take an action. The action you want them to take is to visit the web page created for your home where they can view your home's details and schedule a showing.

This web page is called the "Landing Page". It contains details about the home, photos and embedded video or 3D tour if available. All of your marketing is aimed at getting buyers to go to this web page. On this page, they see details about the home and about local schools, a walk score and a map of the area. If we are holding the house open, the dates and times of the open house are listed. Buyers can schedule a showing right on this page, download a flyer or request more information. Visitor activity is tracked on this page, so the number of potential buyers that have seen the home's details is known. How the viewer found the page is also known which allows the effectiveness of the advertising to be tracked.

The Facebook ad should be targeted to a narrow audience. This is one of the most powerful features of Facebook advertising. Instead of just broadcasting your home to millions of people, most of whom are not interested, your ad can be delivered to users that are more likely to be interested. When we create and ad, we narrow the audience to the age group that is most likely to buy the home. If the community is age 55 and over, presenting the home to 20 some things won't be very productive.

Next, a geographic area is selected so that anyone currently in the area has a chance to see the ad. Finally, the target audience is narrowed to those who have shown specific interests such as "buying a home", "new home", "property search" and so on. Careful selection of the target audience will get your home in front of interested home buyers.

Facebook ads can also be displayed in Instagram. Instagram tends to have a younger audience than Facebook and therefore may not be as effective as Facebook for selling your home in certain areas or for certain homes. We continually test market our ads and review their effectiveness. In our area at this time, Instagram has not proven as effective as Facebook. Your mileage may vary.

YOUTUBE

YouTube has about 1.9 billion users. While not exactly a social media site, it has many similar features such as the ability to Like a video, leave comments and follow video channels. You can leverage your videos on YouTube as a content resource for emails, web pages, flyers and Social Media, and you can take advantage of YouTube's search engine to get your home seen by potential buyers.

The videos you've created can be uploaded to YouTube, and then embedded in web pages and emailed to your friends and your Realtor's contact list. When a video about your home is posted to YouTube, use the address of your home as the title. This will help users find your video when they search for your home by address online. The Lifestyle Narrative will be the source for the video description and a link to the home's landing page should appear in the description.

YouTube Fun Facts

- 35+ and 55+ age groups are the fastest growing YouTube demographics (these are home buyers!)
- People watch 150 million hours of YouTube every day
- 60% of people prefer video platforms to live television
- 20% of users leave a video if it hasn't hooked them in the first 10 seconds
- YouTube is technically the second largest search engine

YouTube is the perfect place to post a virtual tour of your home. We often create a teaser video for the 3D interactive tour designed to entice viewers to view the full interactive tour. Even if your Realtor is posting videos to their YouTube channel, you should post or share the same videos to your own YouTube channel. Your home will gain added exposure from being listed on 2 channels and sharing a link to your own channel will help to entice your friends to visit your channel and reshare the video with their friends.

PINTEREST

Pinterest works differently than Facebook. It is designed around images that you save ("pin") in collections called "boards". Pins have a much longer lifespan than Facebook posts. Pins that you create may show up in search results or on your follower's pages years after you originally created them. This is like the billboard strategy of Facebook ads, but it happens organically.

A categorized board can provide another channel in which potential buyers can find your home. Pinterest also has an advertising option in which, like Facebook, you can target specific demographics. Ads are called "Promoted Pins". We haven't yet found promoted pins to be as valuable as Facebook ads when it comes to home sales.

You can create a board for your home on your own Pinterest site, but if your Realtor has a Pinterest account, posting to their board may provide you with wider coverage. They may be able to share the board with potential buyers and other Realtors. When you create the board, the Lifestyle Narrative should be the source for the board's description.

The board should be named something like "Home for Sale: [your address]". Then you can go to your Realtor's web page for your home and using the "Pin It" button in your web browser's toolbar, pin the photos of your home to your board.

Write a short description for each room and add appropriate hashtags such as:

    #homes
    #forsale
    #lakewoodranch
    #sarasota
    #florida
    #pools

If you don't have the Pinterest "Save" or "Pin It" button, visit this link to install it:

    https://about.pinterest.com/en/browser-button

What is a hashtag? A hashtag is a word or phrase preceded by a hash mark (#), used within a message to identify a keyword or topic of interest and facilitate a search for it. The site will index the post by the hashtags and used properly they help users find your post on Social Media sites. Examples: #realestate #sarasotahomes

---

VIRTUAL STAGING

When a home is empty and has no furnishings it often doesn't present well online. On one hand, the home isn't cluttered, and buyers aren't distracted by taste-specific furniture or wall-hangings. On the other hand, it can be more difficult for buyers to envision living in an empty home than in a home that is tastefully furnished. One solution is to hire a professional stager, an option we discussed earlier. Another option is to Virtually Stage the home.

Virtual Staging uses special software to place 3D models of furniture, rugs, artwork, decorative plants and other furnishings "into" the photographs of a home. The end results are close to reality when well done. There are several services that provide Virtual Staging tools online and some will do all the work for you. Choose the level of service you require. If your Realtor offers Virtual Staging (and if not, ask them why not), have a look at some examples in their prior listings.

When we virtually stage a home, we begin by carefully selecting images of the home best suited for the process and that showcase the featured rooms. The photos are uploaded to the Virtual Staging software and calibrated. Calibration involves carefully aligning verticals and correcting for perspective. Once calibrated, the room is ready for furnishing.

The software provides furniture and accessories in a various styles and colors. An item of furniture is placed in the room, scaled and positioned in the "3D" space. Artwork can be added to walls and area rugs placed under furniture. Just as in real-life staging, less is more.

Not all Multiple Listing Systems may allow Virtual Staging. Our local MLS only recently began to allow it and we must add a disclaimer informing the viewer that a room has been virtually staged. Ask your Realtor if your MLS allows it. If not, it can still be used on the Realtor's website or in other media such as flyers or advertisements.

DON'T FORGET MOBILE

Most buyers are using mobile devices in their search for a new home. You can take advantage of this use of mobile devices to gain an unfair advantage on your competitors. If a home doesn't display correctly on their phone or if the photos aren't professional, buyers will abandon the home with a swipe of their finger. Your home, however, can grab their attention and keep it if you follow the advice in this book.

We have a mobile app that we and tens of thousands of other Keller Williams agents provide to their buyers. Your home is listed on this app and buyers can easily find your home. If they are in the area, they can bring up all the homes for sale with touch of their finger and then see inside your home right on their phone. In the near future an upgraded version of the app will provide buyers with expanded information, neighborhood insights, and a lot more.

Any web pages that displays your home is must be mobile-friendly. That means the page will function correctly and look great on tablets and phones, not just a desktop computer screen. Too many Realty websites are still not designed for mobile devices. The technical term for creating a website that works well on mobile and desktop devices is called Responsive Design.

Facebook and Instagram users avidly use their phones and tablets. The Facebook ad must be designed so it displays well on mobile devices. Facebook provides tools that allow us to view the ad on different platforms so we're a sure it will always look great on all devices.

Make sure the landing page linked from the call to action on Facebook or Instagram is mobile-friendly too. If the buyer is taken to a page they can't read on their phone, they'll abandon the page immediately. And don't forget to make certain that email messages display properly on mobile devices.

The good news is that your home can stand out by making everything about your home mobile-friendly and having it available on a mobile phone app. It's one more edge you can leverage.

USING TECHNOLOGY TO TRACK SHOWINGS AND AUTOMATE FEEDBACK

When your home is listed, your agent has several options for allowing buyer's agents to schedule showings. We use an electronic, Internet-enabled lockbox that can only be opened by licensed Realtors or approved vendors (e.g. a licensed home inspector).

Using the electronic lockbox has several advantages over the old combination lockboxes. Whenever a showing is requested, you and your Realtor will be notified. If the home is occupied, you or your Realtor can approve the showing time via a text message. Or you can request for the showing to be scheduled at another time.

Every access into the home via the lockbox is tracked. Your Realtor will know everyone who has entered your home. The system automatically requests feedback from showing agents when the showing is complete. The feedback will be immediately be sent to your agent. At the end of the week your Realtor can generate a report containing the details and feedback from every showing.

The electronic showing system should be set up to make it as easy as possible for buyers to schedule a showing. Requiring 24-hour notice before a showing is not recommended unless absolutely necessary. Buyers and agents will skip over homes that require long lead times. Very often the buyers have only one day available on a weekend to visit homes. They may never get to see your home if they can't schedule a same-day showing.

The best situation is what we call Go and Show. Usually this is only appropriate for vacant homes, but it allows an agent to show a home almost immediately. Keep the lead time for the showing as short as possible. That might mean you need to leave your home on a moment's notice but if the buyer must wait to see your home, they may decide to skip it.

The systems used by some Realtors require a phone call to a call center to schedule a showing appointment. In our opinion this is an unnecessary impediment to getting buyers into your home quickly and easily. Even more inconvenient is when the listing agent requires that s/he receive a phone call to schedule a showing. Agents don't usually answer their phone right away or return calls quickly. If a buyer's agent is trying to schedule an afternoon's worth of showings for their buyer, they may not have the time to wait for a return call. They'll move on to another home that can be scheduled quickly.

Electronic lockbox, web-enabled showing systems aren't free, but they are an important use of technology to help get your home sold. If buyers can find your home on the Internet but have a hard time getting in to see it, all the marketing in world won't help sell your home.

CASE STUDY #4 THE FEIL HOME

Jim Feil came to us and asked if we could look at his home in Sarasota, FL Things weren't going exactly as he planned. The home had been on the market for almost 6 months and received no offers. In fact, it was not attracting much interest at all and had few showings. Jim and his son David needed to sell the home to finance David's recent move to Minnesota for an exciting new job change. After all these months with lackluster activity, they didn't know what to do.

The home was in a beautiful, quiet gated community close to shopping, within 15 minutes of the beaches and downtown, and with fast access to I-75. One challenge was that while most of the homes in this community included a pool, this home did not. The lack of buyer activity was a big concern.

We listed the house and went to work, employing the pro-active marketing techniques in this book to attract agents and buyers to the house. It was worth the effort, for in just 27 days, a buyer made an offer on the house. 31 days later the home closed at the price the Feil's needed to finance David's job change and move to Minnesota.

Here's what Jim had to say about his experience:

"Vicky Ranck saved the day with the sale of our home in Red Hawk Reserve in Sarasota. After getting no offers on the 2012 house for over six months, we replaced our previous realtor and Vicky took over. She immediately began effective marketing of the home and it sold in less than a month at a very good price.

Besides using some new and different marketing approaches Vicky studied the market in great detail and knew how to emphasize the right features. We got lots more interest in the home right away.

She made the process easy for us. She let us know ahead of time all the details we needed to decide on and helped us with each step of the process. She kept track of everything for us and she was always available to talk and answer questions. We will certainly use Vic again"

The moral of this story is: "Marketing Matters".

TECHNOLGY + TRADITIONAL = SUCCESS

Non-technical marketing tools still hold an essential place today, especially when they are married with Internet and Social Media marketing.

Flyers

A well-designed flyer must be created for your home. This flyer should not be the default consumer brochure that a Realtor prints from the MLS. It must be purposefully designed as a marketing piece not just be a list of the facts about the home. The flyer will contain the most relevant photos of the home, excerpts from the Lifestyle Narrative, a list of your home's most important features and a call to action (schedule an appointment, visit the property landing page or view a video). You can email a PDF version of the flyer to friends, coworkers and family announcing the sale of your home. Statistically each person that receives the flyer knows 250 people. That's a lot of potential buyers! The flyer will also be handed to visitors at an open house and to buyers during a private showing. We also send a copy of the brochure to buyers in our database that may be interested in your home.

Direct Mail

A "Just Listed" or "Open House" postcard or trifold brochure sent to 100 neighbors has proven to be highly effective for us. When we hold an open house, we send an invitation to stop by for a visit. The brochure or postcard has photos and copy similar to the flyer, but it is specifically designed to get visitors for the open house. We'll send another mailing if there is a price adjustment. Your neighbors are a great source of potential buyers. They often know someone that likes the area and would be interested in living there.

Email

The open house invitation and property brochure can be emailed to neighbors as an alternative to or in addition to direct mail. Email has the advantage of allowing us to track who has read the email. We email clients and prospects in our database when we list a home. If we know a home fits a buyer's wish list, we'll send them an email, but we will also call them right away.

Phone Calls

Fewer and fewer real estate agents are becoming skilled at the art of pro-active prospecting. A dirty little secret is that most agents fear rejection and that keeps them from picking up the phone and prospecting for their sellers. We find that friendly phone calls to homeowners in the area of the home for sale are effective in getting the message out. When they see the open house sign or receive a post card in the mail, they are more likely to pay attention. Speaking with neighbors also gives us an opportunity to find out what they like about living in the area. This essential information is something we can add to the Lifestyle Narrative and advertising materials.

OPEN HOUSES

One of the first things we do after a listing is live on the MLS is schedule an open house. Many Realtors don't like open houses. They don't like giving up an entire Sunday afternoon sitting in someone else's home. They know that according to NAR statistics less than 3% of homes are sold at open houses. They reason that if 100 people come to an open house, they will only have a 3% chance of selling the home. A single open house may get a dozen visitors on average so the odds of finding a buyer at an open house look slim. Our success rate with open houses is much, much higher and open houses are one of our most effective sales tools. Here's why.

We actively promote the open house online and on Social Media. We create a Facebook ad inviting people to the open house and distribute it starting on Thursday afternoon. Why Thursday? Because Facebook is busiest on Thursday after 1 PM and all day on Friday. More and more often, visitors tell us they found the open house on Social Media, not by seeing the signs along the road. Of course. we put out open house signs and lots of them. We'll put out anywhere from 8 to 16 signs for a single open house. And we invite neighbors to the open house by email, phone or by mail. As we mentioned earlier, neighbors are an important source of potential buyers. Very often they have a friend, co-worker of family member that would like to live in the neighborhood.

We may also do a Facebook Live session from the open house. Live videos tend to get a lot of attention on Facebook and can add a personal touch. They are more informal than other forms of video and grab a viewer's attention because of their casual nature.

When visitors come to the open house, we engage with them and explain the unique features and benefits of the home with excitement. We draw on the Lifestyle Narrative, so we make sure to present the home in the manner it deserves. We have a plan for working with visitors. We don't follow them like a dog, but we don't ignore them either. When I go into a store, I don't mind if a salesperson asks if I need any help. But it annoys me when they pretend to straighten the shelves near me, so they can pounce on me later. On the other hand, it frustrates me if they disappear and I can't find them when I do need help. We are at an open house to work, not read a book or to do crossword puzzles. We make sure that visitors get the right amount of attention at the right time.

David and Victoria Ranck

After the open house, we follow up with visitors and thank them for coming. The home is brought to their mind a second time. And here's the secret that I'm not sure most Realtors understand. When we're at an open house for one of the other properties we have listed, we may find a buyer for YOUR home. We do a lot of open houses and so we meet a lot of buyers. On several occasions we've met someone at an open house and shown them another home later that same day.

We do a lot of open houses because we know they are effective when done correctly. Most of our open houses are held on Sunday or Saturday, but we also hold them during the week from time to time. For example, we may open a house for an hour or two when parents are bringing the kids home from school.

Here are some tips to make sure your home's open houses are as effective as possible.
- Don't stay in the home during the open house. Buyers want privacy and want to be able to envision the home as their own. Let your Realtor be your proxy.
- Before the open house, give it a quick cleaning and straighten things up. Arrange pillows, put dirty dishes in the dishwasher, make the beds.
- Turn on all the lights in the home and open the blinds. Your home shows best when there is a lot of light.

- Don't leave piles of dirty laundry out where they can be seen.
- During warm weather turn the AC down to 72 – 74 degrees. Visitors will unconsciously know that the system is in good working order.
- During cold weather, turn up the temperature so visitors are warm. If you have a fireplace, start a fire to provide an inviting atmosphere.
- Lock pets in their cages or better still, take them with you.
- Bake cookies before the open house. The enticing smell will conjure an image of "home" to buyers. And I like cookies!
- Make doubly certain the entry way is clean and shows well.
- Personally invite your neighbors to the open house and tell friends and co-workers about it. Send the open house flyer your Realtor created to neighbors and friends by email or hand it out at work.

PLAN THE WORK, WORK THE PLAN

Marketing your home starts with a plan. Putting a sign in the yard and listing the home on the MLS is not a plan. If your home is to effectively reach potential buyers, you must go a lot further than the MLS. We put our marketing plan in writing so we can apply it to each property we list. We've written it down, but it is not static. Because the market is constantly changing, we continually update our marketing plan and customize it for each home.

"Our jobs as marketers are to understand how the customer wants to buy and help them to do so." - Bryan Eisenberg

---

Here's an outline of the plan we use to market homes. We customize the plan and choose the activities that will be most effective for each home. Let this serve as a guideline for your home's marketing plan.

Pre-launch Phase

Our marketing plan begins before the home even reaches the market. We call this the Pre-launch phase, and, in many ways, it is the most important step of the entire marketing campaign. It sets up and supports the entirety of the marketing activities that follow. Each property gets a customized version of the plan that will best promote the home to the right audience.

- The listing agent performs a walk-through of the home, taking notes that will provide input into the Lifestyle Narrative and assist in staging the home
- The lead marketer and listing agent create the "Lifestyle Narrative" showcasing the home, the property, the location and the neighborhood
- The marketing copy is created from the Lifestyle Narrative
- Professional Photos are ordered
- 3D video is ordered if appropriate
- Professional staging is ordered if required or desired
- The home is "edited" with the owner's assistance to make sure it looks its best in photos and in person
- Changes are made that will help the home sell such as repairs, minor upgrades, painting, etc.
- Often, additional staging elements are added such as decorative wash towels for the baths, place settings or centerpieces in the dining room
- A PDF flyer is created which will be sent to potential buyers, given to the homeowner and used at open houses

Launch Phase

The home is prepped and staged. A photographer has taken professional photos and created a virtual tour and/or video. We have composed a compelling Lifestyle Narrative and extracted the listing description from it. Now it's time to get it onto the MLS and open it up for the world to see. One tip: double check the listing after it is live to be sure there are no mistakes in the details.

- The listing details are uploaded to the MLS along with the photos and video.
- The listing is activated on the MLS.
- A landing page is created showcasing your home and enticing buyers to request more information or schedule a showing
- A Social Media ad is created that showcases your home with a slideshow or video. The ad links to the landing page. This ad will run for about 30 days.
- The professional photos are used to create a virtual tour which is posted online.
- The virtual tour is uploaded to YouTube.
- The listing is shared with the big syndicated sites like Zillow and Realtor.com from the MLS
- We share the listing on over 350 additional sites like Military.com, Investor Loft, eReal Investor and Frontdoor.
- Your home is sent from the MLS to buyers that are looking for a home like yours. Realtors have set up saved searches that email newly listed homes to their clients when the homes have the features desired by their clients.

- We contact buyers in our database that we think will be interested in your home. Sometimes this results in a very quick sale.
- We schedule the first open house for your home.

Ongoing Marketing Activities

Once the home is active on the MLS and we have completed the initial marketing activities described above, it's time for the ongoing portion of the marketing campaign. We employ a combination of open houses, Social Media posts and ads, Facebook Live, YouTube, direct mail and old-fashioned phone calling to promote your home.

- The Social Media ads continue to run
- We hold one or more open houses
- We create a social media ad for an upcoming open house
- We invite neighbors to the open house by one or more of the following
  - Emailing the flyer to neighbors
  - Mailing an open house invitation to neighbors
  - Calling and personally inviting the neighbors to the open house
- We broadcast a Facebook live video from the open house
- When another agent's buyer marks your home as a favorite, we contact the agent and encourage them to schedule a showing

- When another agent shows the home, they are automatically contacted with a request for comments
- If we do not receive comments after a few days, we contact the showing agent directly and ask for the buyer's thoughts about the home
- Each week we review the results from the previous week's marketing and adjust as needed. If an ad isn't getting the views or click-throughs we think it should, we'll reword it or change the photos

30 Day Review

If a home hasn't had many showings or no offers in 30 days, we'll review the marketing activities and look for ways to increase buyer engagement. It is likely that it is time to discuss a price adjustment with the homeowners. The market sets the selling price of a home and if there have been no offers after 30 days, the market is probably telling us the price is too high.

When a price adjustment is made, we create a new Social Media campaign announcing the price change and we notify agents whose buyers have shown interest in the home. We'll schedule and market a new open house.

The ongoing marketing then continues as before with the new price. In some markets, 30 days is too long to wait to make a price adjustment. Your local market might require that you make an adjustment much sooner.

KEY TAKE-AWAYS

- The best way you can make your home stand out above the competition is by following these guidelines

- Quality photos, videos and other marketing materials are vital in today's world of Internet users with short attention spans

- Leverage Social Media like Facebook, Instagram and YouTube to find buyers where they are

- Combine technology with other marketing techniques for the best effect

- Make sure your marketing is suitable for mobile devices

- Open houses work well if they are done correctly

David and Victoria Ranck

HOW TO CHOOSE A REALTOR

A Partner with a Vested Interest in Your Success

"Navigating a real estate purchase is tricky business... there's no substitute for an experienced professional. A crack negotiator who knows the market can save you time, money and heartache ... playing hardball when necessary—and staying on top of the process."
– Time.com (Everyday Money)

How do you choose the right Realtor to sell your home? Now that you've read this book you should have a good idea of what to look for in a Realtor. The best Realtor for you is not always the first one you talk to or the one you meet at an open house. Your home is one of your largest investments. Take time to carefully find the Realtor that is best for you.

A smart Realtor has a vested interest in your success. After all, if they can't sell your home, they don't get paid! But they should also have an emotional investment in your success. Victoria once told me "When a home has been on the market for too long, it keeps me up at night." You want to hire a Realtor that really cares about you and your success.

Here are some thoughts on how to interview a Realtor for the job of selling your home.

FIND THE RIGHT REALTOR FOR YOU

Most homeowners select the first Realtor they talk to or they use a Realtor recommended by friends, family or co-workers. Recommendations are an important indicator to consider but they shouldn't be the only factor in your decision. What worked for your friend's home may not work for you. They may really like the Realtor as a person but being likeable alone does not make a Realtor competent at their job.

80% of homes are sold by 20% of Realtors (it's amazing how that 80/20 ratio applies in so many areas). You want to hire one of the 20%. Make sure that the Realtor you choose is an *active* Realtor. If they are a "part-time" Realtor, they may not have the bandwidth, tools or expertise to give you the service that you deserve.

We suggest that you interview a few Realtors before hiring one to sell your home. Your goals are to find out if they are up-to-date on what it takes to sell your home in today's market and if they are a good fit for you and your family. It is important that you feel comfortable with your Realtor and you are convinced they will work hard to help you meet your goals.

Important Note

Do not choose one agent over another simply because he or she suggests a higher list price for your home. Real Estate Agents don't set the selling price for your home, the market does. If an agent suggests a price far above the price of similar homes that have sold, ask them to explain in detail what it is about your home that commands such a high price. Insist that they back their claim up with facts and figures.

After you've selected a few candidates the next step is to schedule an in-person meeting. Allow at least one hour to show the agent your home, discuss a pricing strategy and find out how they plan to sell your home. Here are some of the most important topics you'll want to discuss.

INTERVIEW TOPICS

Personalized CMA

Did the agent come to the interview prepared with a professional quality Comparative Market Analysis? If not, just move on to the next candidate. If they haven't taken the time to do research to win your business, how hard will they work for you to sell your home? How much thought was put into the CMA? Is the Realtor just comparing superficial features like number of bedrooms, square feet and inclusion of a pool or are they comparing upgrades, condition, location, architectural features and other qualitative features?

Recommended Sales Price

Review the agent's CMA. Does it include similar homes that have sold, are under contract and are currently for sale? Did the agent select homes that have similar features and amenities? Did the agent tell you what price to set for your home? Or did s/he work *with* you to arrive at a price? Even when the agent knows what the list price should be, the fact that they engage you in the decision can be a telltale that they will partner with you to sell your home. Never choose an agent solely because they suggested the highest listing price. Anyone can say they can sell a home for more than it's worth and it is an easy way for an agent to get a seller to sign the listing agreement. The market will always correct an unreasonable price downward later.

Market Knowledge

Did the agent exhibit a knowledge of the local market? What do they know about your community? Ask the agent how the local market is doing. Can they provide you with a market report? Do they know the average list price to sales price ratio in your area? Knowledge of that ratio will help you set your asking price and factors into the net sheet.

Net Sheet

Did the agent discuss the amount you may expect to net at a given sale price? This is called a net sheet. It is an estimate of your net take-away when your home sells at a certain price after all expenses have been deducted such as doc stamps on deed, closing costs and the agent's commission. We often work up a net sheet at different sales prices to help the homeowner choose the listing price that is best for them.

Seek First to Understand

Did the agent talk "at" you or did they ask questions of you? Did they ask you to explain your goals in selling your home? Did you feel listened to? A good agent is great at asking questions. They'll do their best to understand your situation and why you want to sell now. You might be under a time constraint and need to sell quickly which will affect the pricing and marketing strategy. Or you might have a financial situation that requires that you walk away from the closing table with a certain amount in your pocket.

Marketing Plan

We just reviewed the techniques we know are important to successfully market a home in today's world. Ask the agent to show you their marketing plan. Is it written down? Why do they think it is appropriate for your home? Is the plan concrete and organized or does it seem they are improvising a response to your question? Do they incorporate Social Media advertising? How will they monitor results and make needed adjustments?

Photos and Video

Ask the agent how they produce photos for the MLS and other marketing materials. Do they hire a professional photographer, or do they take photos of your home on their smartphone? If they use their smartphone, move on to the next candidate. Seriously, professional photos are that important for your home's life online! Do they have a custom virtual tour (slideshow) created for each home? Will they create video for your home? If your home is a good candidate, will they have a 3D interactive tour created?

Prep Work

Has the agent suggested any prep work you need to do before listing your home? A knowledgeable agent will provide specific advice on what will make your house more marketable. They may suggest changes to the furnishings, painting walls a neutral color or other simple things you can do to spiff up your home. If they have suggested nothing, ask them what you should do to make your home easier to sell. Why didn't they take the lead and make the suggestions?

Communication

What is their communication plan? When and how do they provide updates to you? Did they ask you for your preferred communication method (phone, email, text)? Are they easy to get hold of? How are you notified of showings and provided feedback from showings?

Commission

Don't start here! You get what you pay for so find out what you get for your money before you talk about commission. A good agent will also be a good negotiator and will help you get the best price for your house. If the agent's commission is a lot lower than other agents you are interviewing, you might wonder why. Are they going to spend as much on marketing your home as the other agents? Another thought: if they need to lower their rate to win your business, how good of a negotiator will they be when your money is at stake? If their rate is higher than the other agent's rates, ask them to support the higher rate with tangible reasoning.

Experience

Has the agent been in Real Estate for at least a few years? If not, don't reject them outright but take a close look at how they plan to market your home. Frankly new agents can sometimes be very hungry and work extremely hard for their clients. That said, experience counts for quite a bit. An agent that has "been in the business" for 30 years could be out of touch with the current market. Don't let years in business alone make your choice for you.

Finally, Do You Have a Connection?

All other things being equal, you want to work with someone that "clicks" with you. Real Estate is a relationship business and it is important to feel comfortable with your Realtor partner. Transactions can be tricky and there are almost always bumps along the road. Having someone you trust and believe in will remove some of the anxiety when these bumps occur. You should feel that you can be completely candid with your Realtor and ask them anything.

WHAT ABOUT OFFERS LIKE "IF I DON'T SELL YOUR HOME, I'LL BUY IT!"

I know of Real Estate agents, good agents that make these kinds of offers. I also know that they seldom, if ever, buy a home from a client. Invariably there are severe limitations on when and how the offer can be claimed. Read the fine print. It may be a requirement that the seller buy one of the agent's listings or the agent may take sole control over the price of the home. S/he may automatically reduce the list price every week or 2 weeks until the home sells. Many homes may not qualify for the offer because of strict requirements. If an agent has an offer like this, make sure they also meet the criteria we discussed above.

KEY TAKE-AWAYS

- Don't just use a Realtor recommended by friends, family or co-workers

- Interview several candidates and ask the questions listed here

- Ask the Realtors to show their marketing plan to you

- Look for a Realtor that you have a connection with, one that instills confidence in you and that will partner with you

FINAL THOUGHTS

Putting It All Together

"Bit by bit, putting it together...
Piece by piece, only way to make a work of art.
Every moment makes a contribution,
Every little detail plays a part.
Having just the vision's no solution,
Everything depends on execution,
Putting it together, that's what counts."

— *Stephen Sondheim,*
Sunday in the Park with George

Stephen Covey said *"Synergy is what happens when one plus one equals ten or a hundred or even a thousand!"*. Selling your home in today's market requires a synergy between You and Your Realtor, and Social Media Marketing and Tried-and-True Marketing Methods. Effective marketing of a home today is best accomplished when every piece of the puzzle works together in harmony. Solo players are at a distinct disadvantage.

Technology can help you win the competition with other homes on the market but it won't be effective if it is not coupled with proper pricing, the enhancement of your home's condition and features, and making sure your home presents well. Don't skimp on photos or videos. For best effect digital marketing must be strongly supported by open houses, mailings, email, phone calls and other "old world" techniques.

For more information and additional tips visit us on the web at:

www.VictoriaRanck.com

REFERENCES

The following sources were consulted or quoted from in the writing of this book:

7 Seconds. (2017). Retrieved from Tribute Media:
https://www.tributemedia.com/blog/you-have-7-
seconds-what-a-visitor-should-know-about-your-
website-within-moments

Everyday Money. (n.d.). Retrieved from Time.com: Source:
http://time.com/money/collection-post/2792049/do-
i-need-a-real-estate-agent/

Keller, G. (2013). *The ONE Thing: The Surprisingly Simple Truth
Behind Extraordinary Results.* Bard Press; 1 edition.

Levine, M. (2012). *Logic and Emotion*. Retrieved from
Psychology Today:
https://www.psychologytoday.com/us/blog/the-
divided-mind/201207/logic-and-emotion

Microsoft's CEO: 80-20 Rule Applies To Bugs, Not Just Features.
(2002). Retrieved from CRN:
https://www.crn.com/news/security/18821726/microso
fts-ceo-80-20-rule-applies-to-bugs-not-just-
features.htm

(2008, 2017). *MLS Statistics*. Realtor Asoociation of Sarasota and Manatee.

Mobile Fact Sheet. (2016). Retrieved from Pew Research Center: http://www.pewinternet.org/fact-sheet/mobile/

(2018). *Profile of Home Buyers and Sellers 2018*. National Association of Realtors.

(2017). *Profile of Home Staging*. National Assocation of Realtors.

(2017). *Real Estate in a Digital Age 2017*. National Association ofRealtors.

Remodeling 2018 Cost vs. Value Report. (2018). Retrieved from Remodeling: www.costvsvalue.com

(2017). *Remodeling Impact Report*. National Association of Realtors.

Sales Enablement Is In The Eye Of The Buyer. (2018). Retrieved from Forbes.com: https://www.forbes.com/sites/forbesbusinessdevelopm entcouncil/2018/10/31/sales-enablement-is-in-the-eye-of-the-buyer-how-to-train-your-reps-with-buyers-in-mind/#3d0cc07f1094

Sellers: The Benefits of Staging Your Home. (2018). Retrieved from HGTV: https://www.hgtv.com/design/real-estate/sellers--the-benefits-of-staging-your-home

Social Media Use in 2018. (2018). Retrieved from Pew Research Center: http://www.pewinternet.org/2018/03/01/social-media-use-in-2018/

Top 20% of Americans Will Pay 87% of Income Tax. (2018). Retrieved from Wall Street Journal:

https://www.wsj.com/articles/top-20-of-americans-will-pay-87-of-income-tax-1523007001

Understanding The Comparative Market Analysis. (2013). Retrieved from Realtor.com: https://www.realtor.com/advice/sell/understanding-the-comparative-market-analysis/

YouTube by the Numbers. (2018). Retrieved from Omnicore: https://www.omnicoreagency.com/youtube-statistics/

Some images courtesy Vecteezy.com.

ABOUT THE AUTHORS

 **Victoria Ranck, Realtor, CPC, SFR**
Victoria is an experienced residential and commercial real estate professional with a broad range of clients from first-time home buyers searching for their dream home to commercial investors seeking to maximize their investment dollars. Her peers have christened her "the numbers girl" – she knows how to make the numbers work for her clients in any price range.

On the Personal Side:

"My first memories are of looking out to sea from our house on the Thames River in New London, CT. From there, I could see Fishers Island Sound, Long Island Sound, Ledge Light, Race Rock and the Atlantic Ocean! My dad and I boated and fished in them all! There began my love affair with all things related to the sea. I suppose it was inevitable, my grandfather was an Azorean Portuguese fisherman who emigrated here

when he was very young. He instilled his love of the sea in his children and my father passed it on to me.

I have continued that love affair with the sea here in Sarasota. From Sarasota Harbor, past Bird Key, through Big Pass to the Gulf of Mexico, the beauty and the wonder here delight me on a daily basis. It has been my pleasure to work with people from all walks of life in a broad range of price points to find them their very own dream home near the water – nothing is far from the water in Sarasota!"

 **David Ranck, Realtor, Marketing Specialist**
David is an experienced Residential Realtor who brings over 25 years of business and Internet marketing experience to the Real Estate industry. Before joining Victoria in Real Estate, David had a successful career as a Software Architect. He was Chief Technology Officer at Software Consortium in Towson, Maryland and Application Development Manager at The Hartford Insurance Group in Connecticut. He brings his knowledge and experience of Internet Marketing and Systems to the Victoria Ranck Group. A fun fact about David is that he helped design the software for one of the first Internet-enabled Multiple Listing Services in the U.S.

> *"I know that less than 3% of home sales today come from traditional advertising. Internet, mobile and social media advertising are among the most effective tools we have to reach potential home buyers today."*

On the Personal Side:

David enjoys composing orchestral music. You can hear some of his compositions on his personal website www.daveranck.com. He is also an amateur photographer and videographer.

HOW MUCH IS YOUR HOME WORTH IN TODAY'S MARKET?
Get a free automated Market Analysis of your Florida home sent to your inbox:
http://bit.ly/get-my-cma

You can contact Victoria and David by email from this web page:
http://VictoriaRanck.com/contact/

David and Victoria Ranck

You can find additional articles and resources on our website:

www.VictoriaRanck.com

www.ingramcontent.com/pod-product-compliance
Lightning Source LLC
Chambersburg PA
CBHW071307220526
45468CB00001B/297